# Under the sea

# "A WORLD OF COLORS."

Discover the Amazing Underwater World with "Under the Sea: A World of Colors" Immerse yourself in the beauty of the ocean with our unique and exciting coloring book. This book is much more than just a coloring book; it's a window into the magical underwater world that will leave your young explorers amazed and educated.

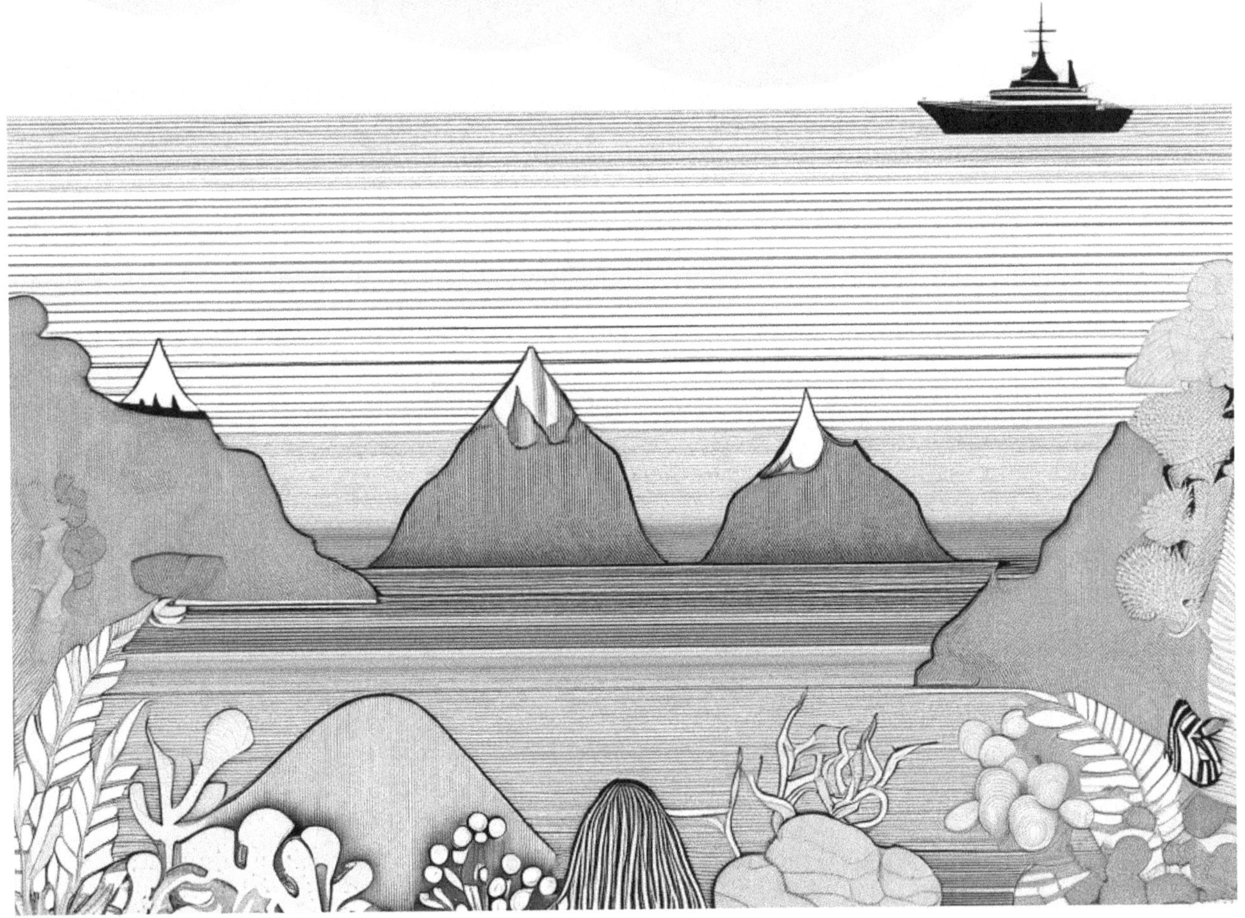

# THIS BOOK BELONGS TO:

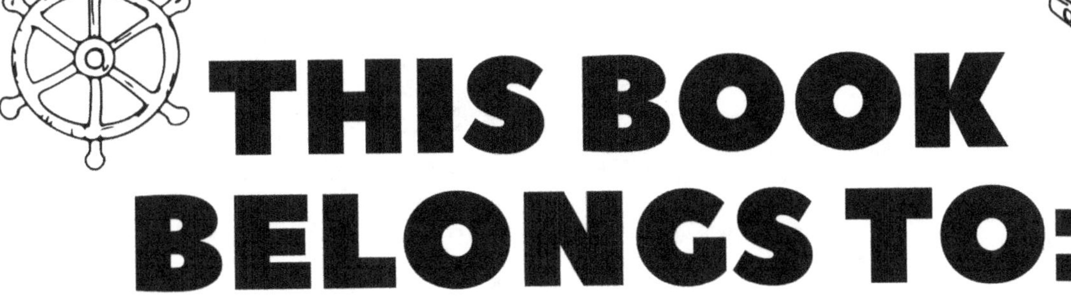

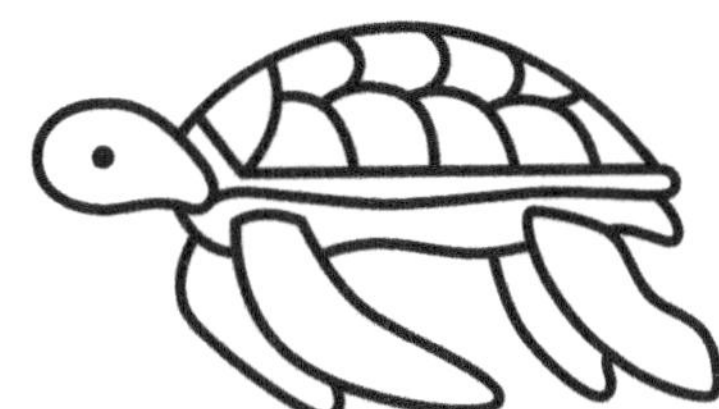

# ESTE LIBRO PERTENECE A:

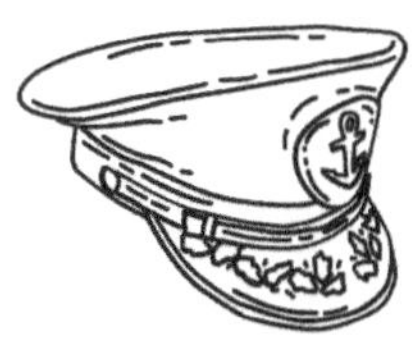

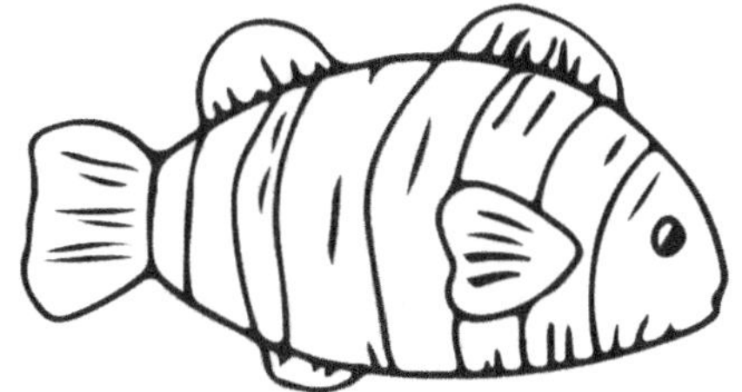

# Mermaid

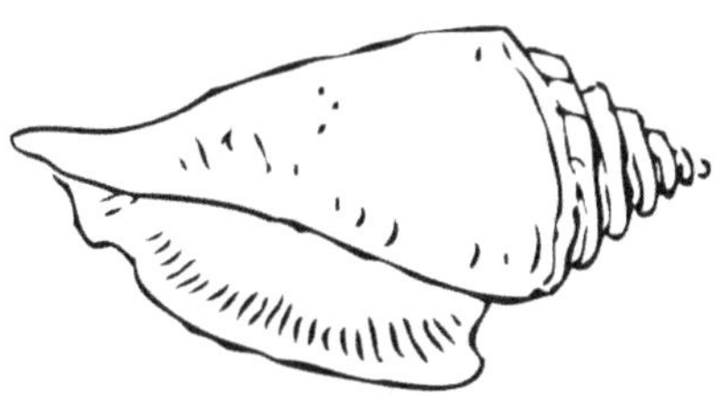

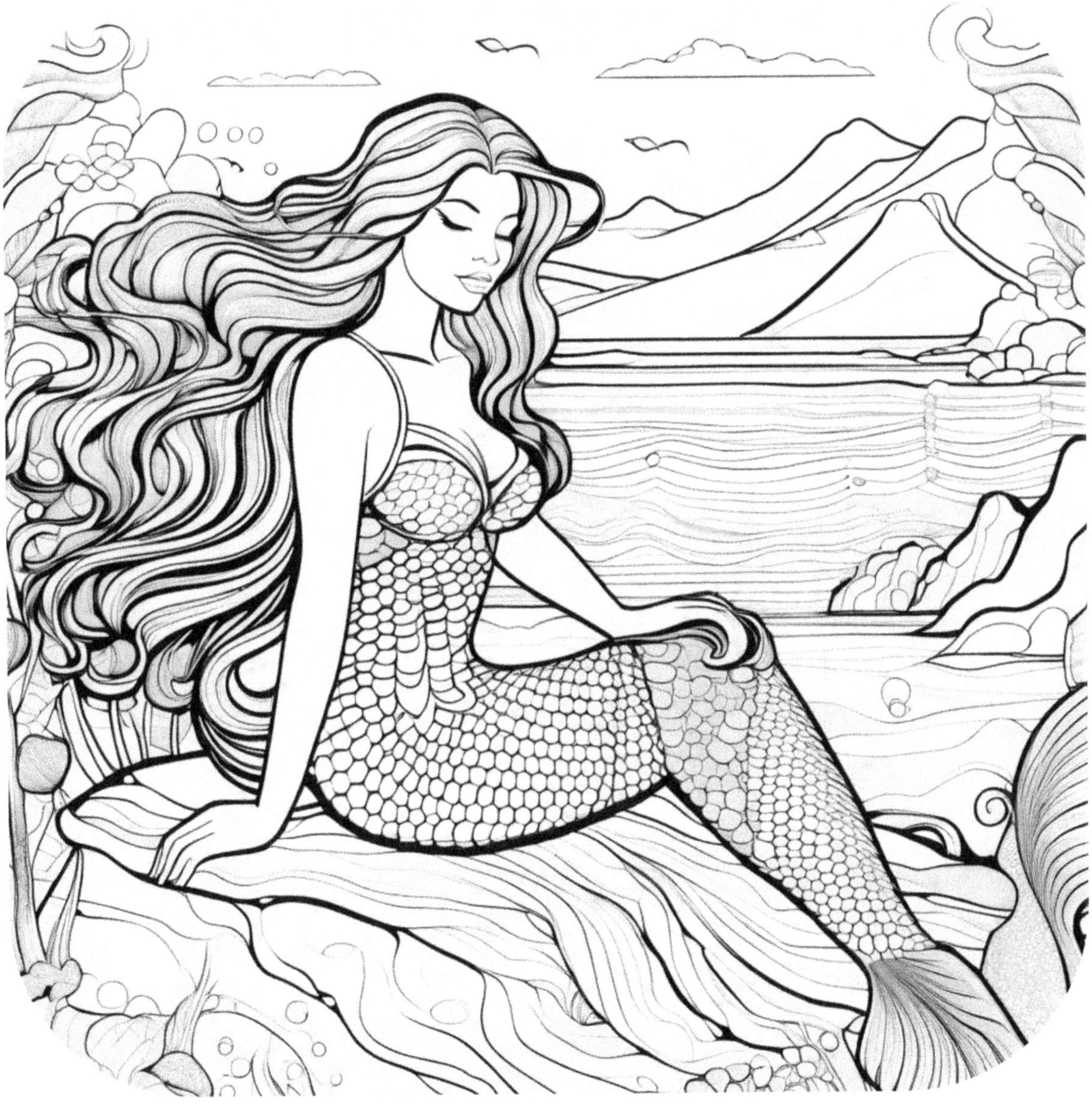

# Sirena

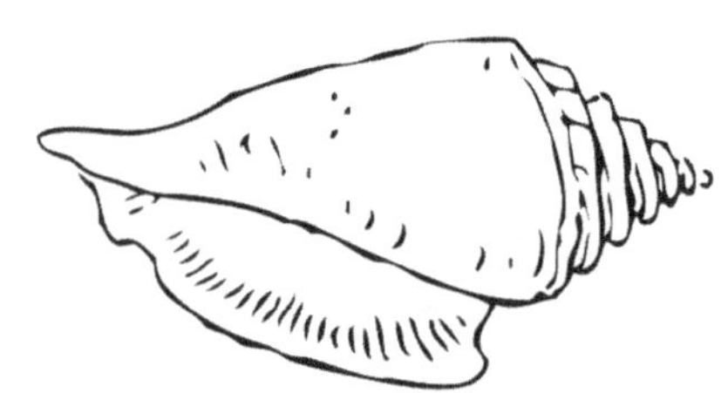

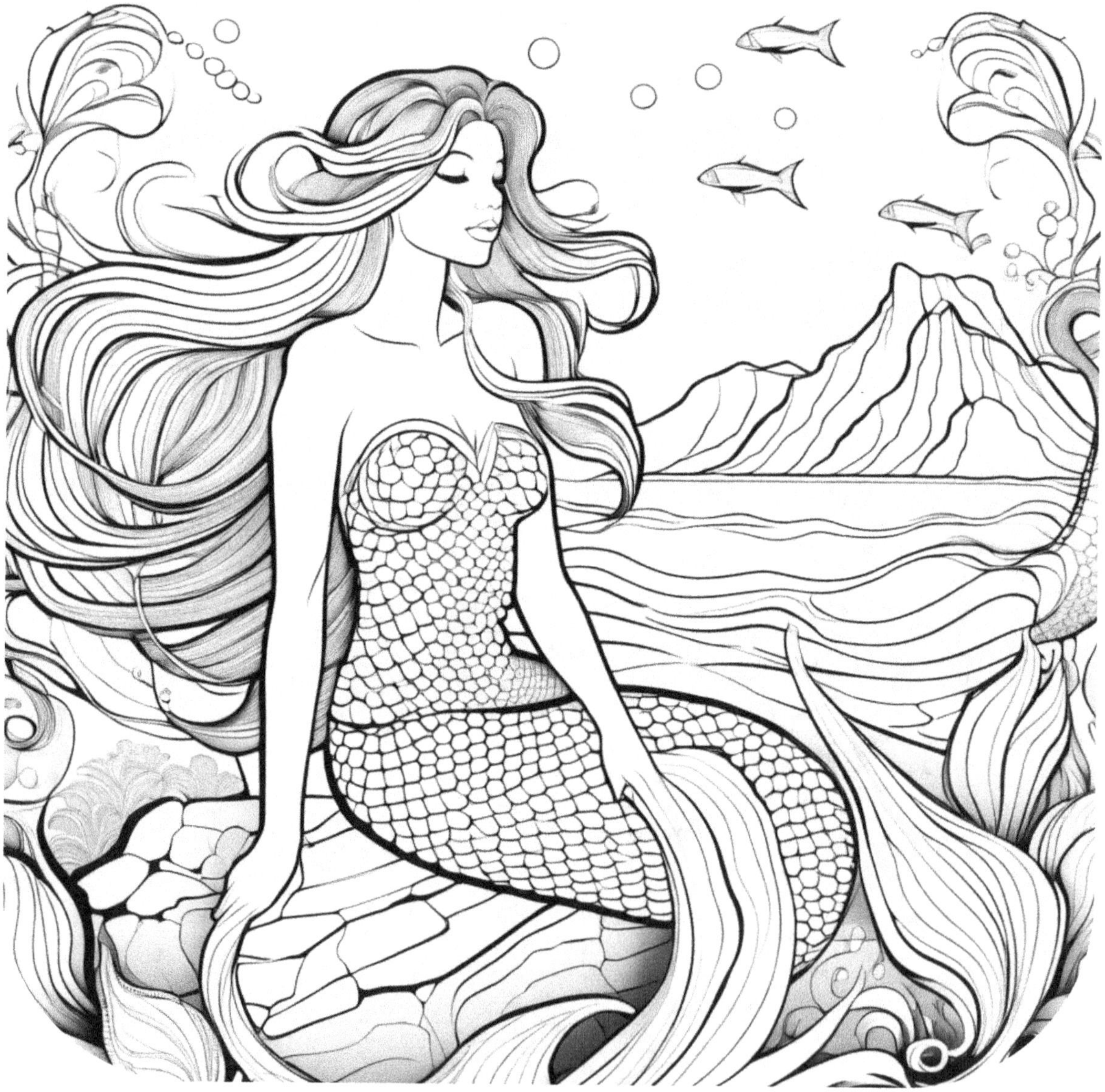

# Little marmaid

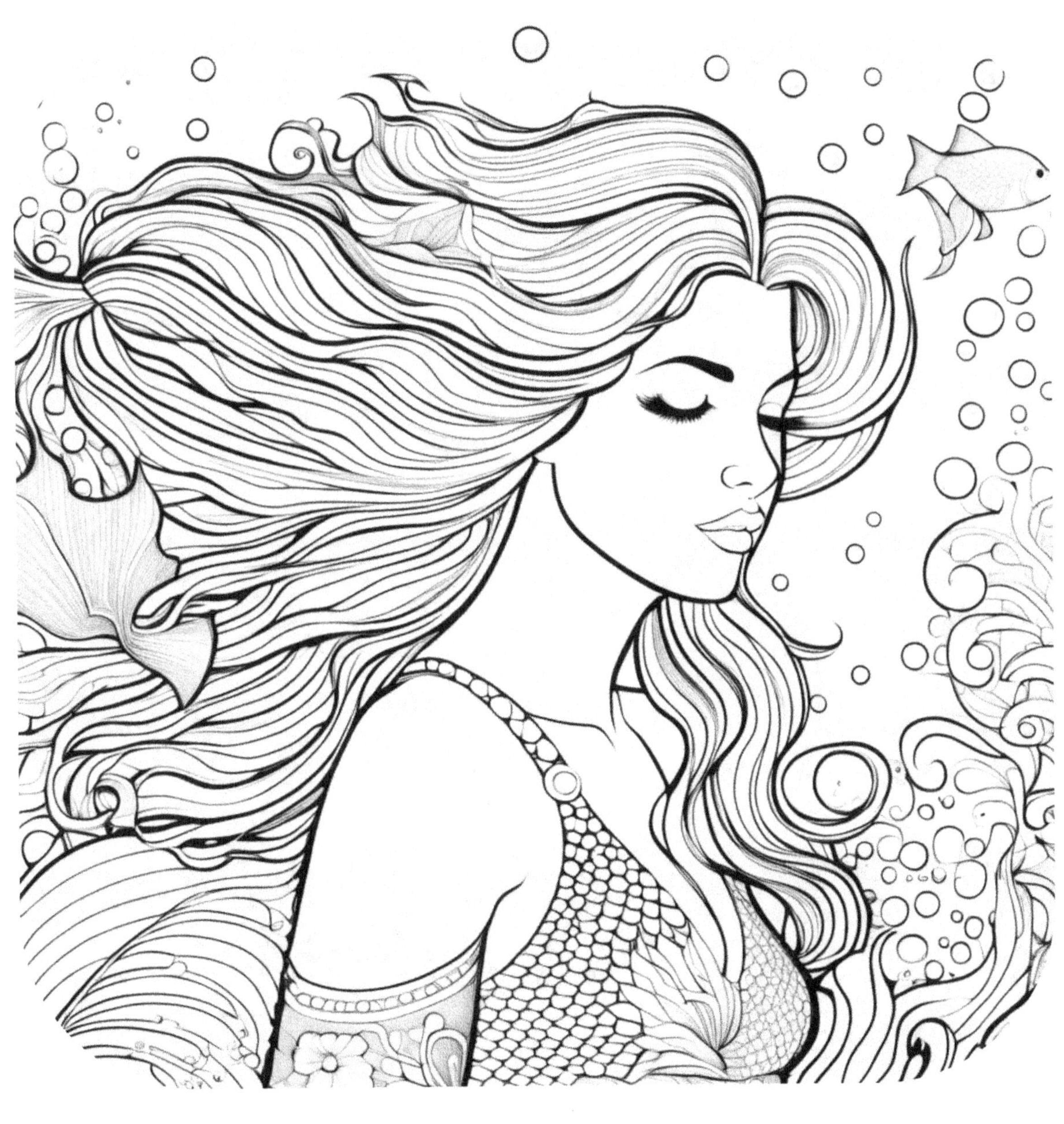

# Sirenita

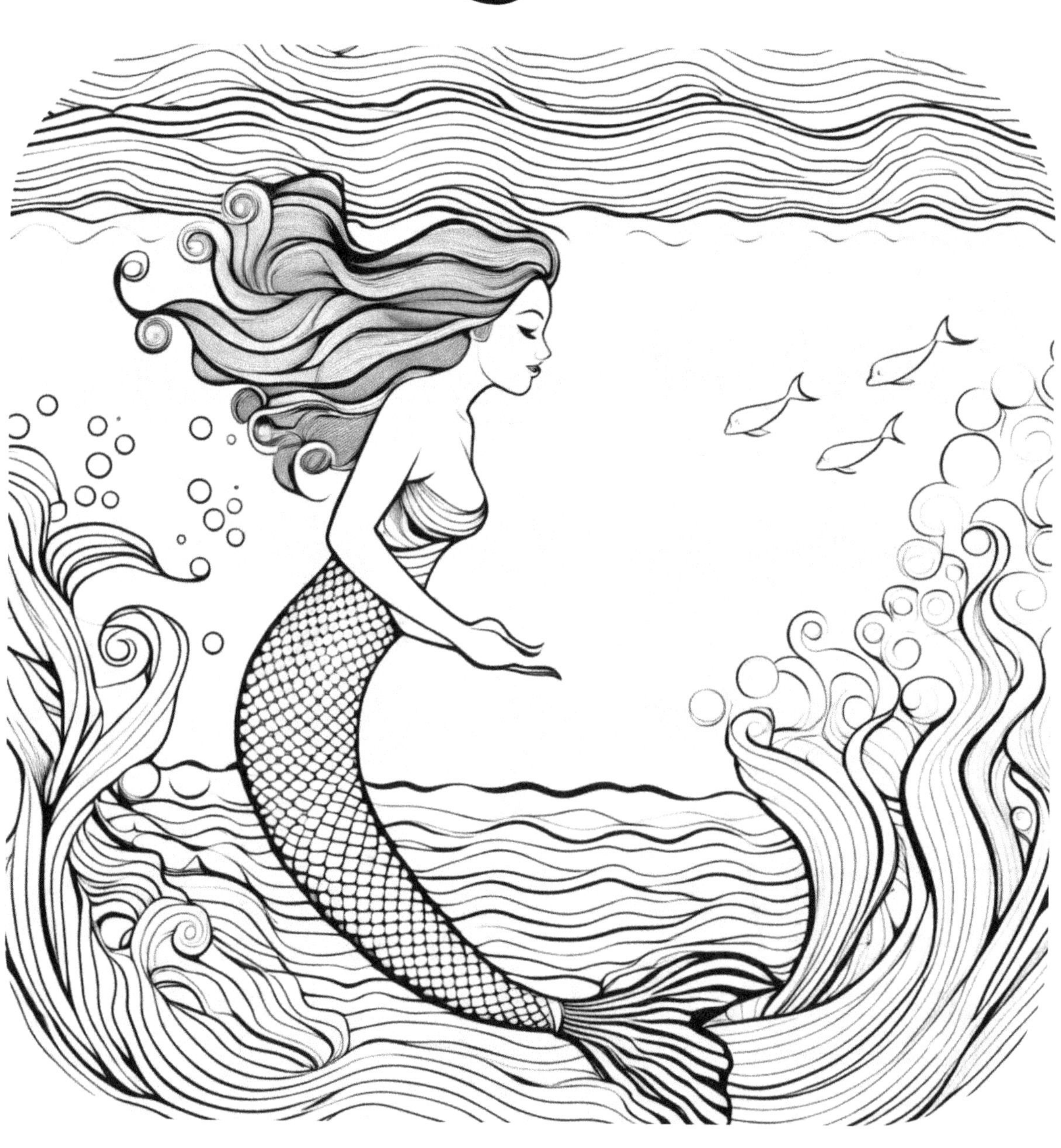

# Dolphin

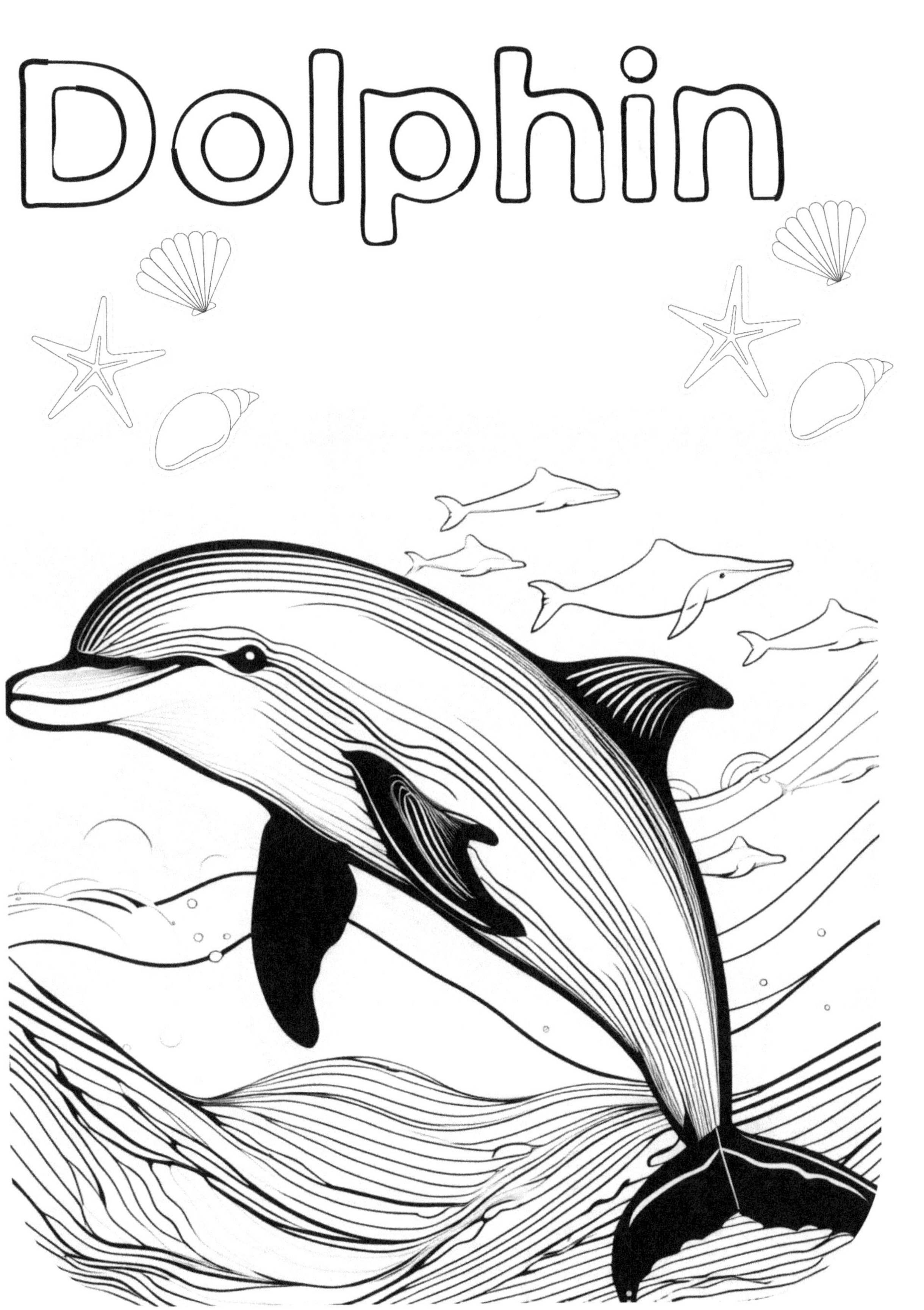

# Delfín

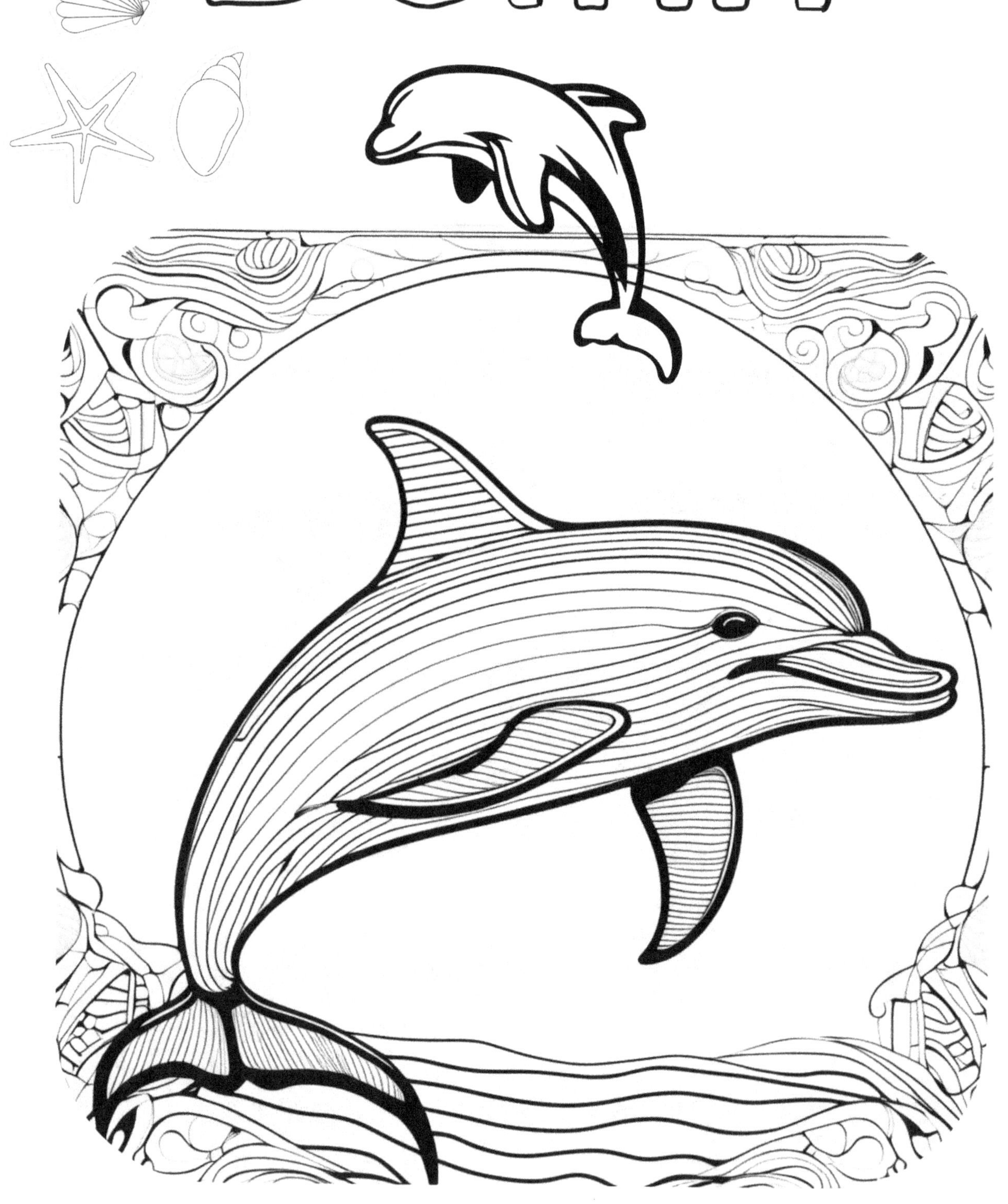

# Starfish

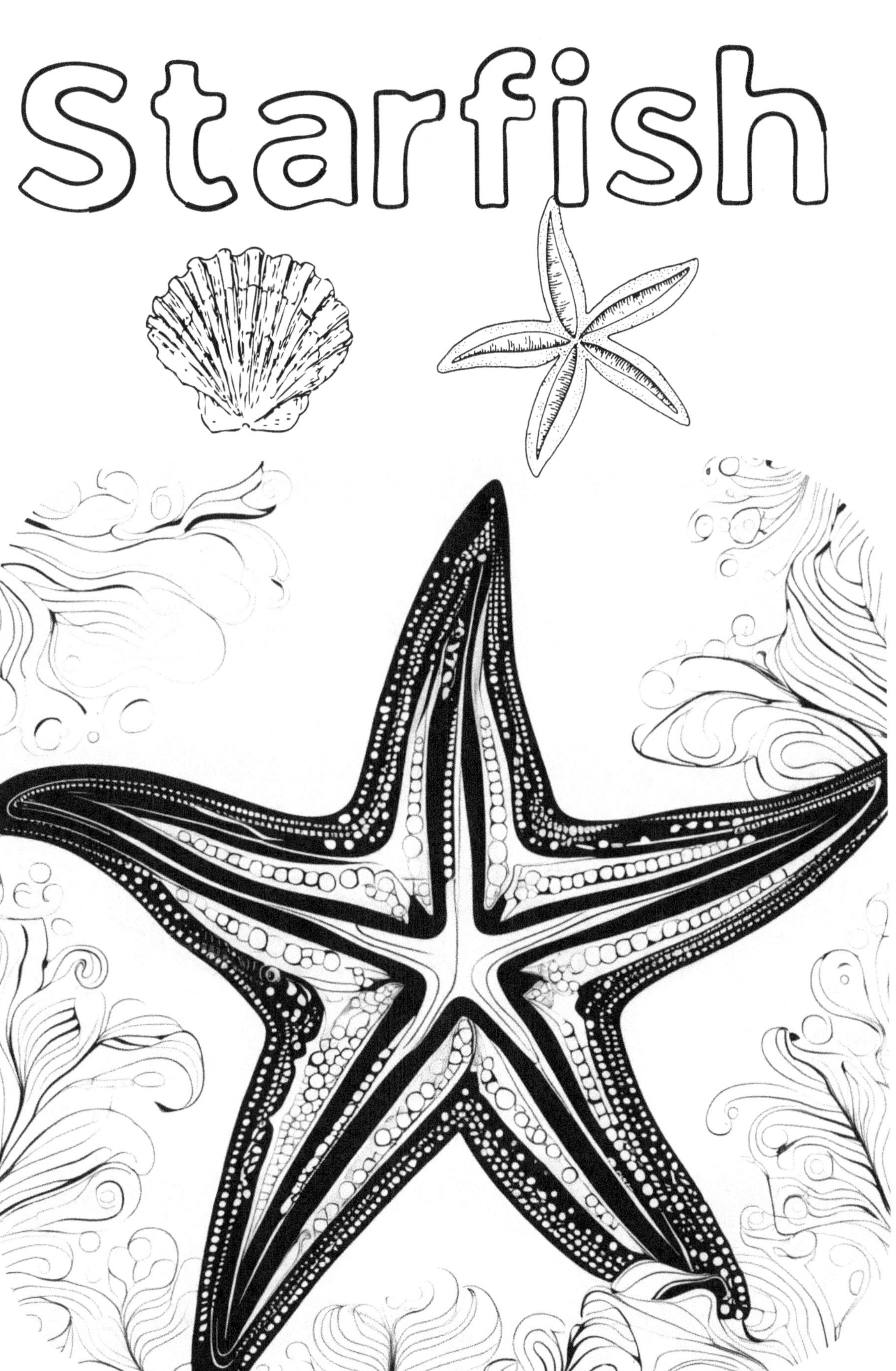

# Estrella marina

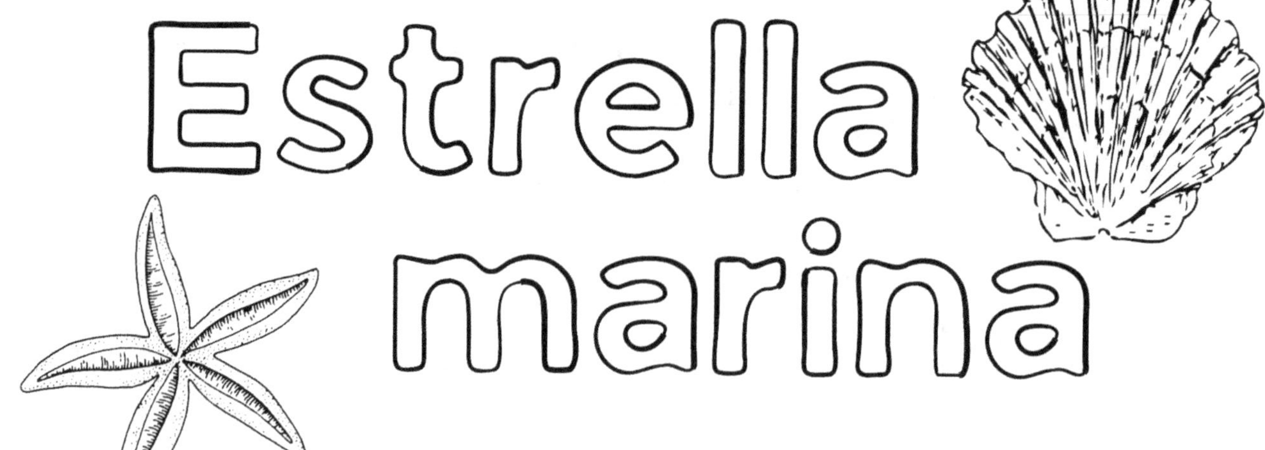

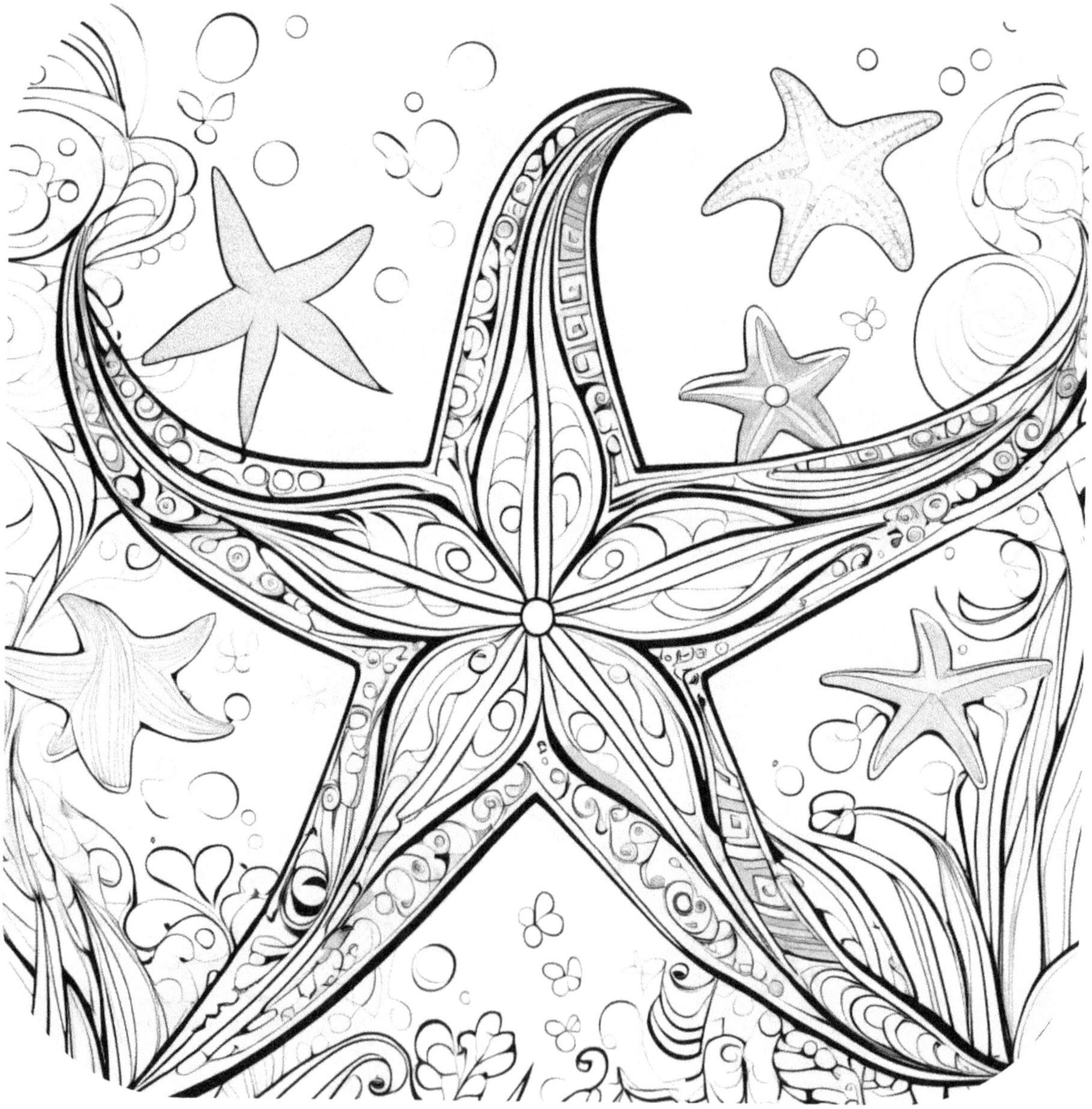

# Sea horse

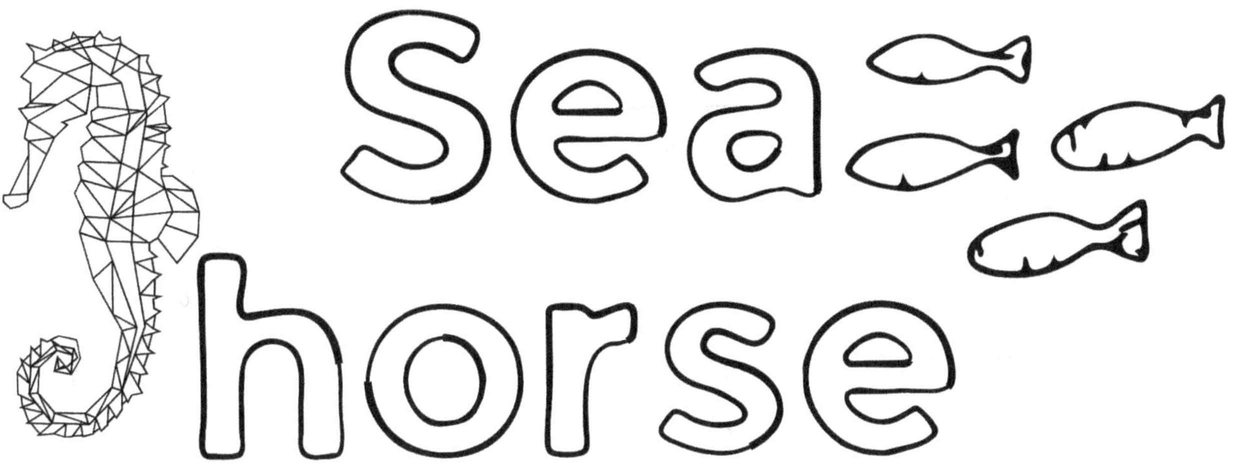

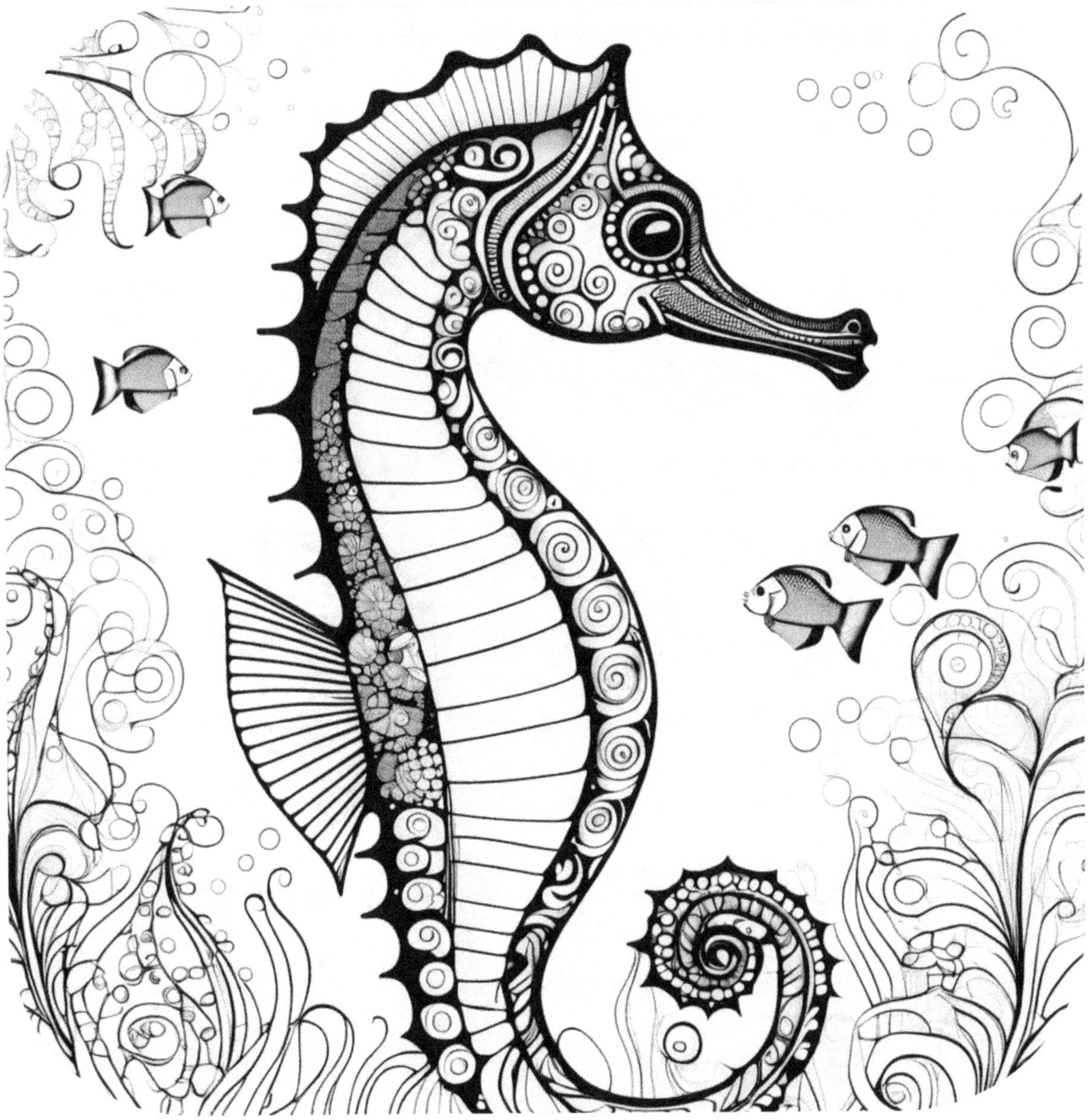

# Caballo marino

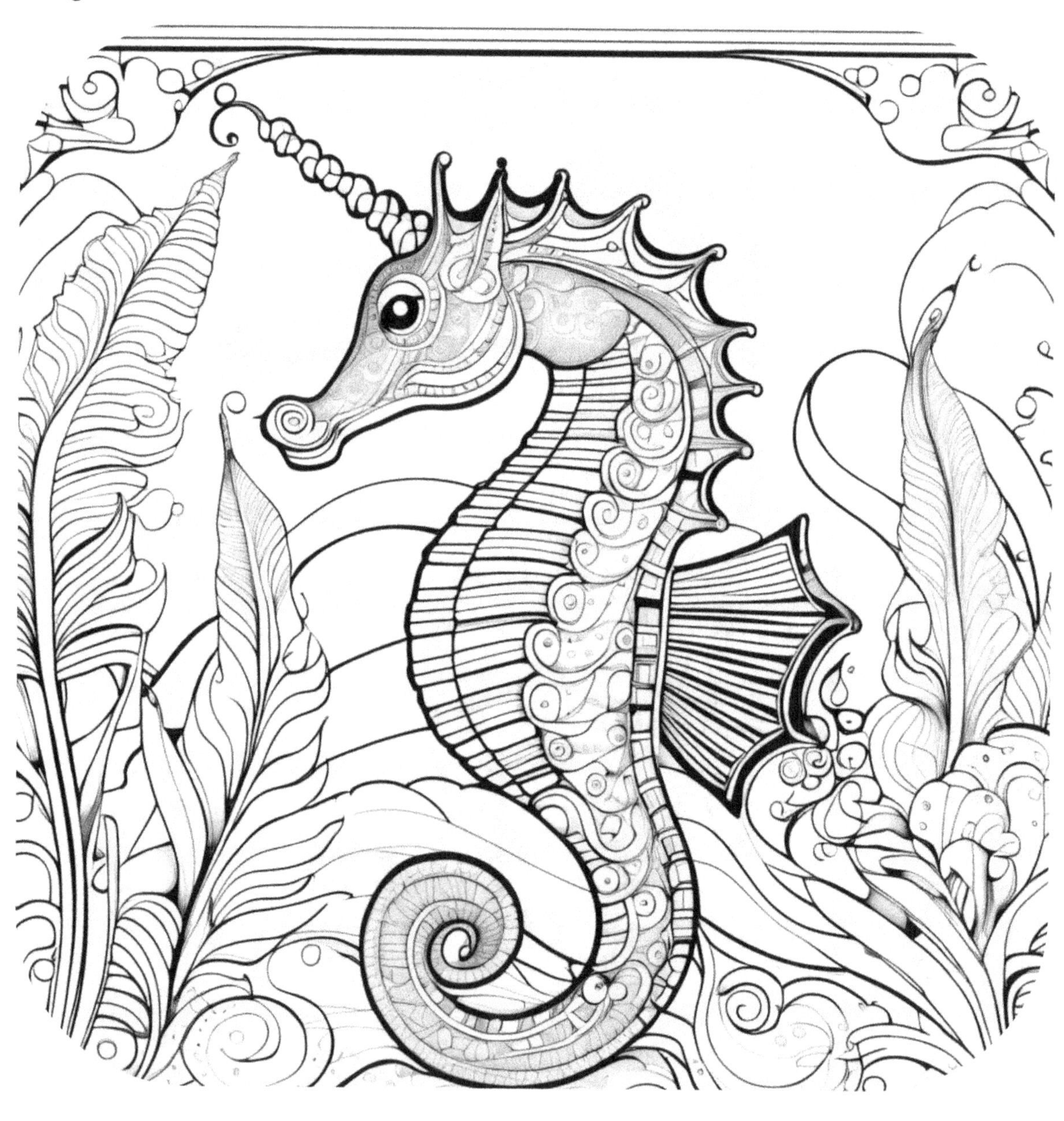

# Shark

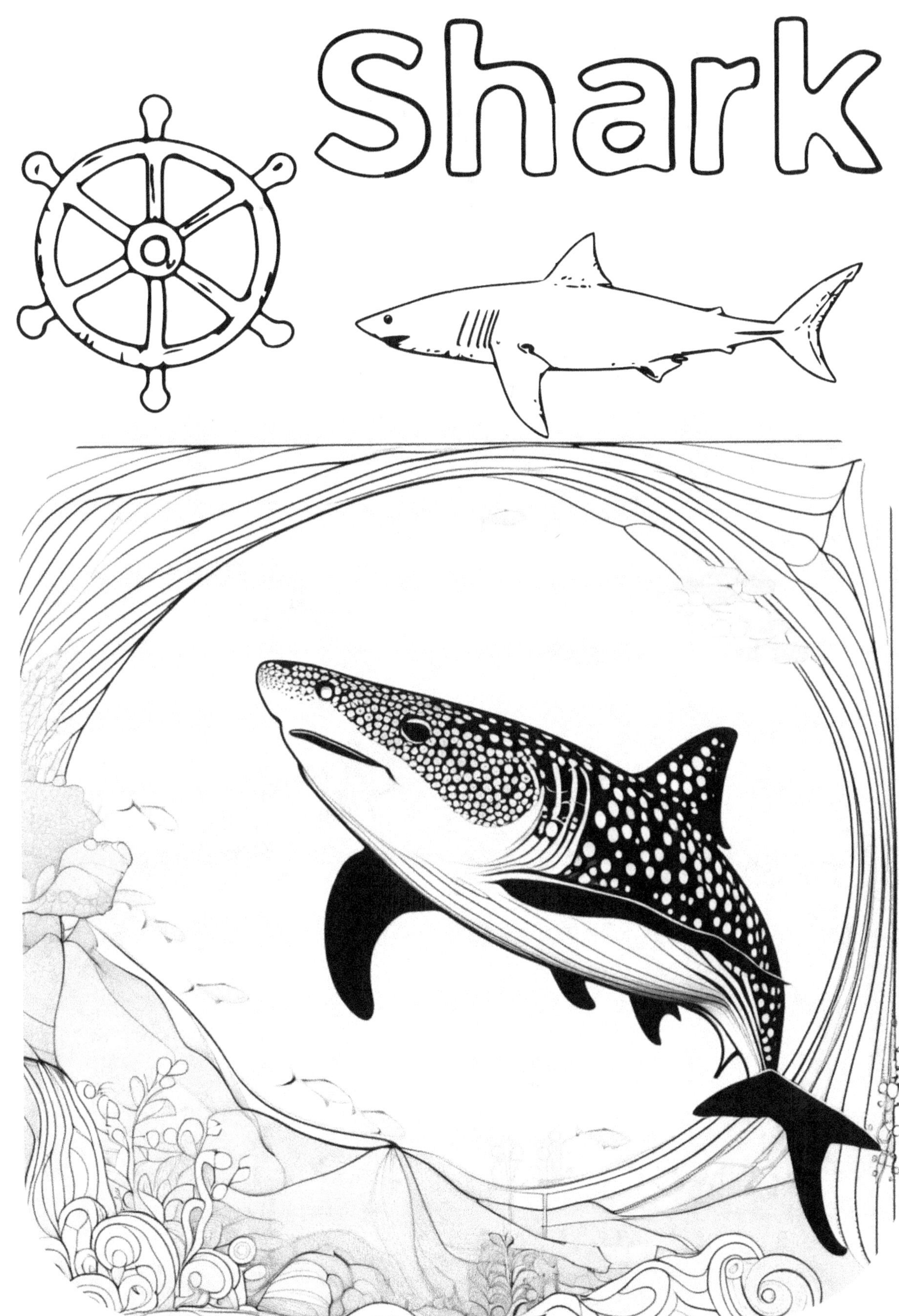

# Tiburón

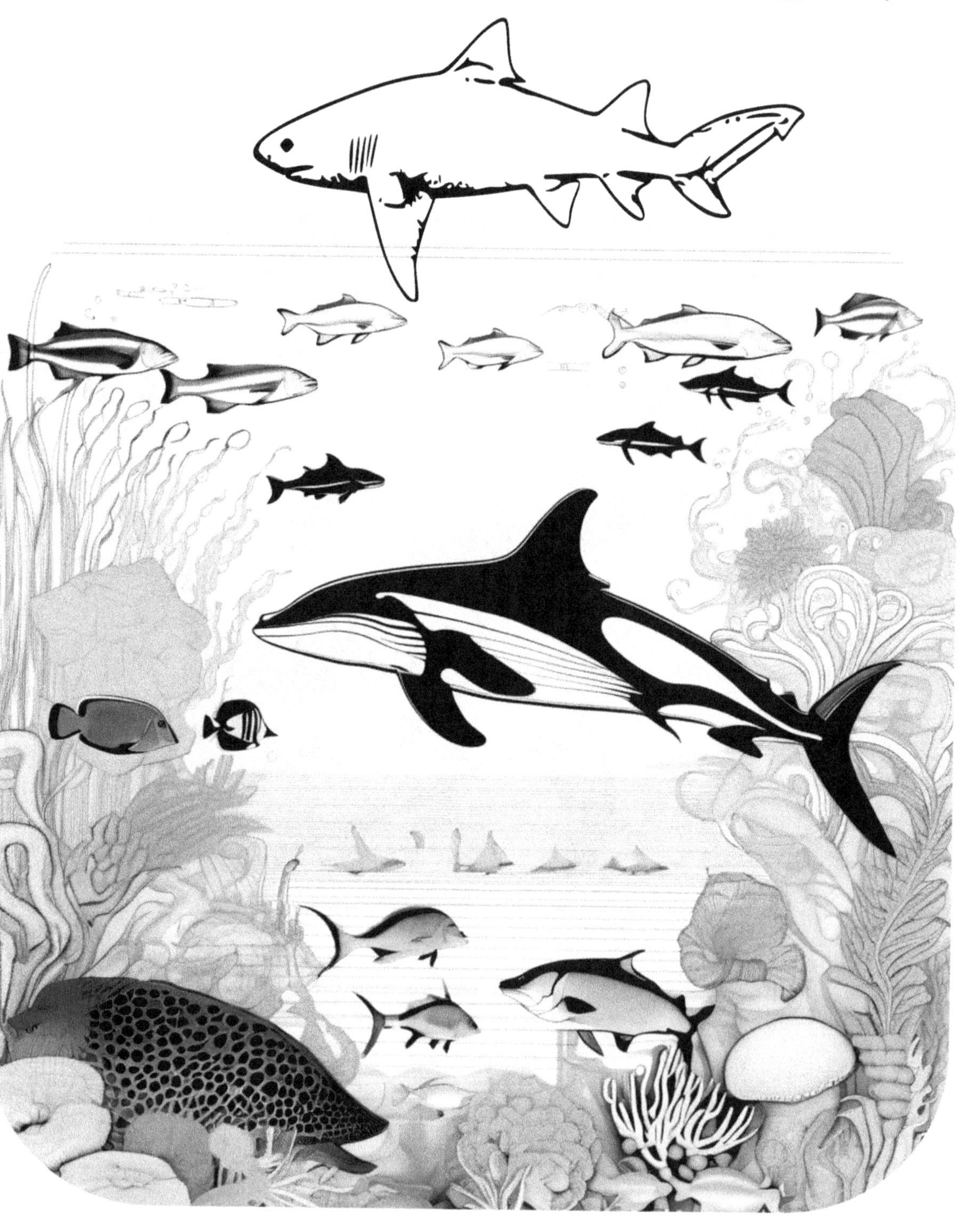

# Shark

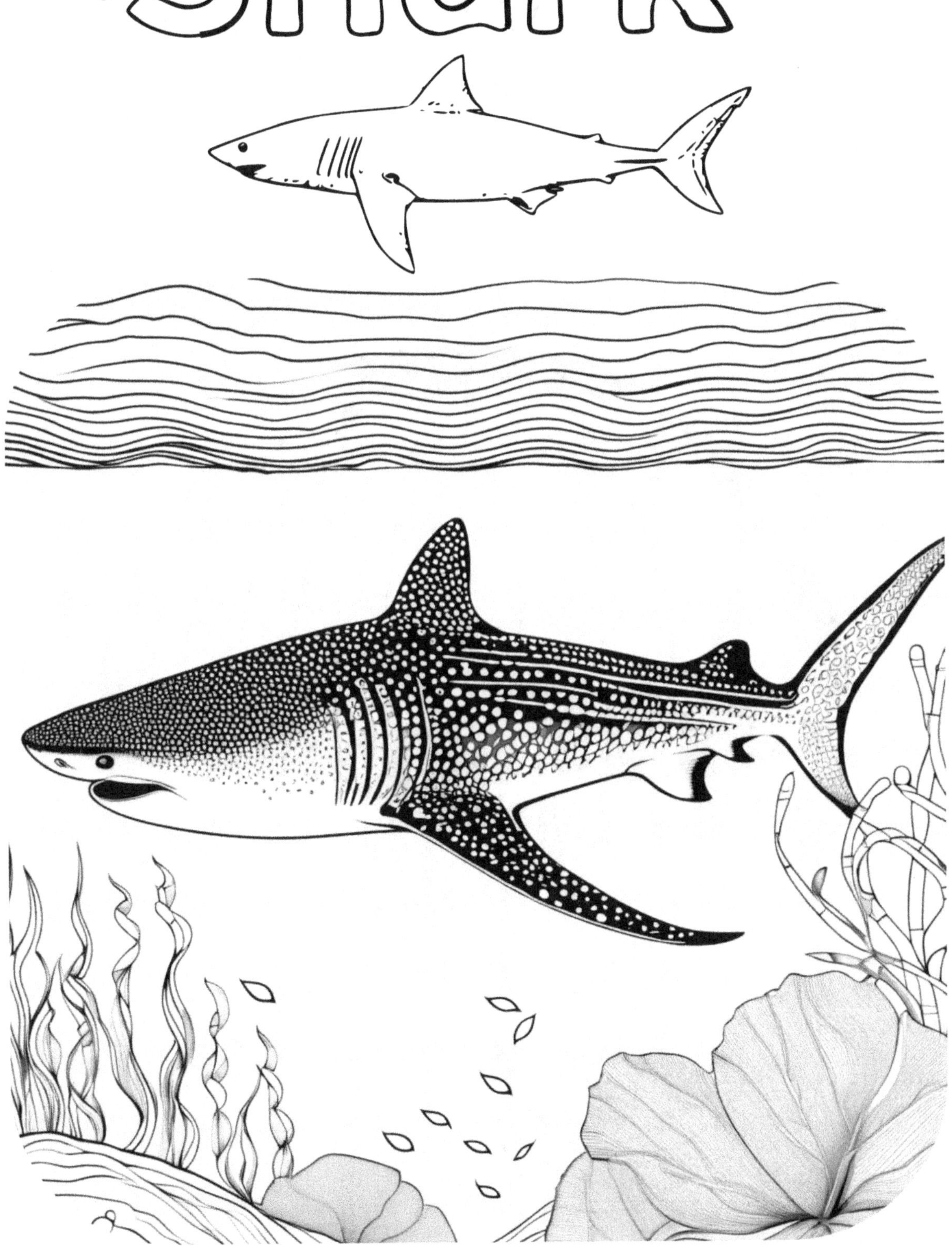

# Jellyfish

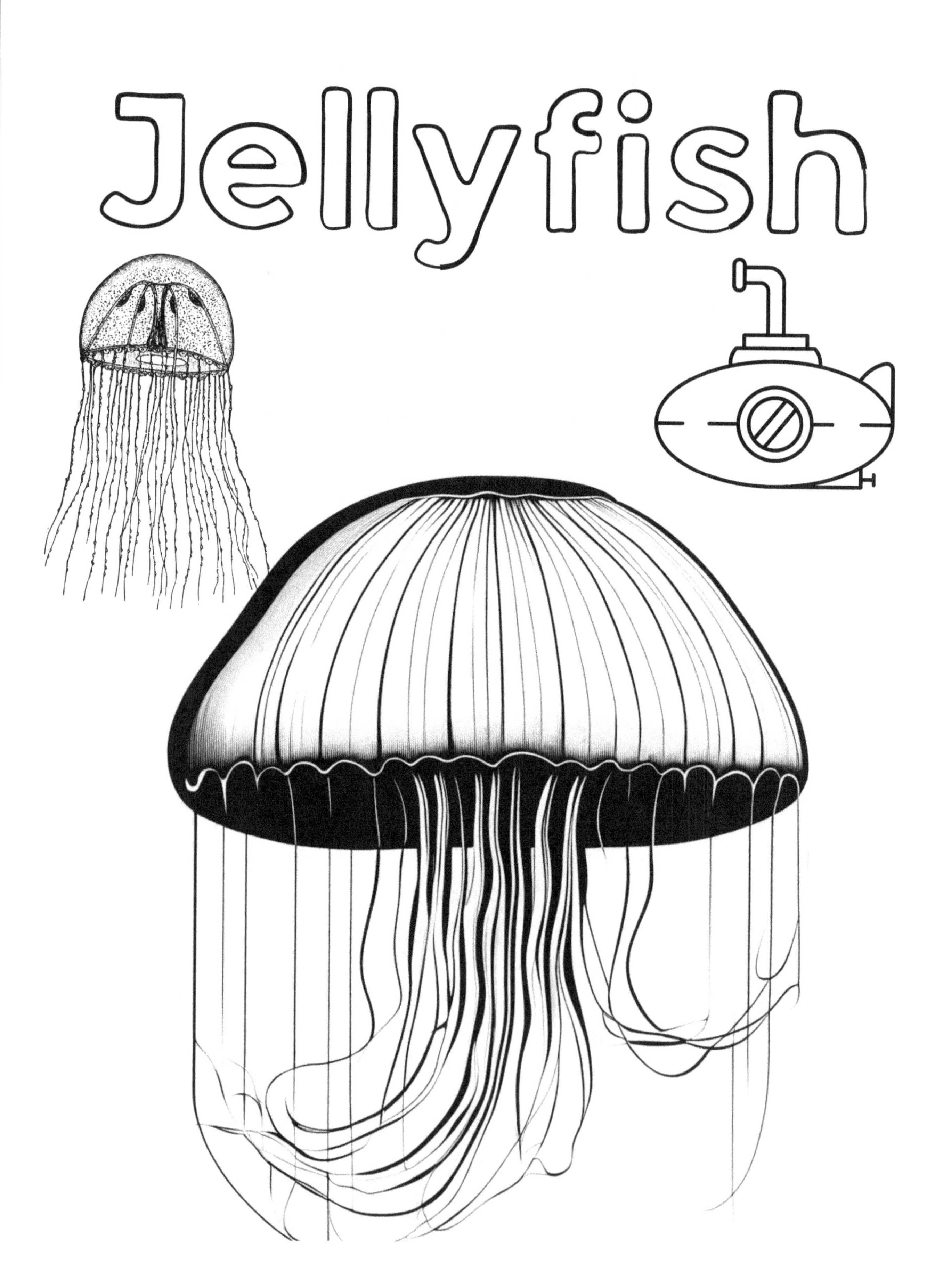

# Medusa

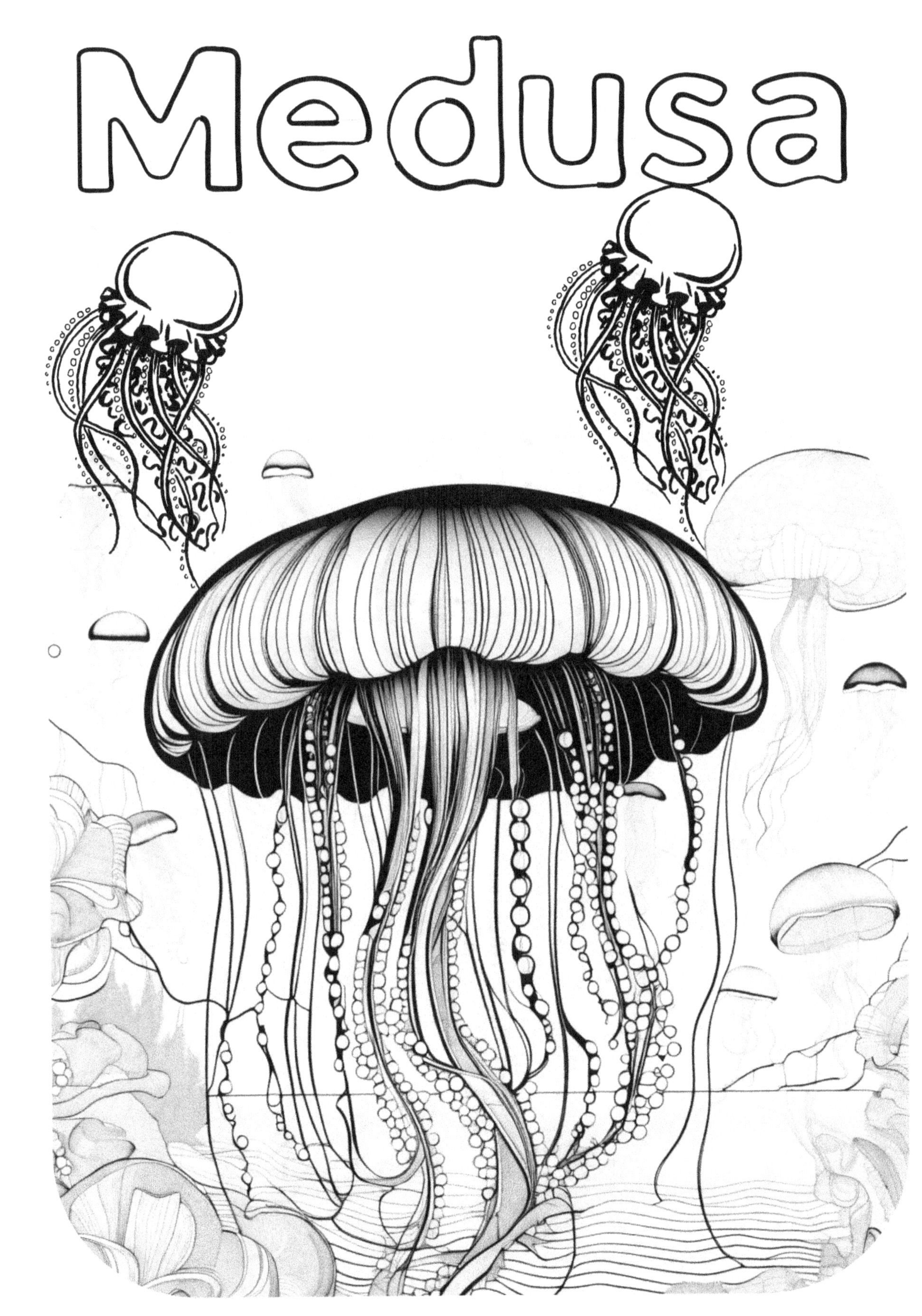

# Fish

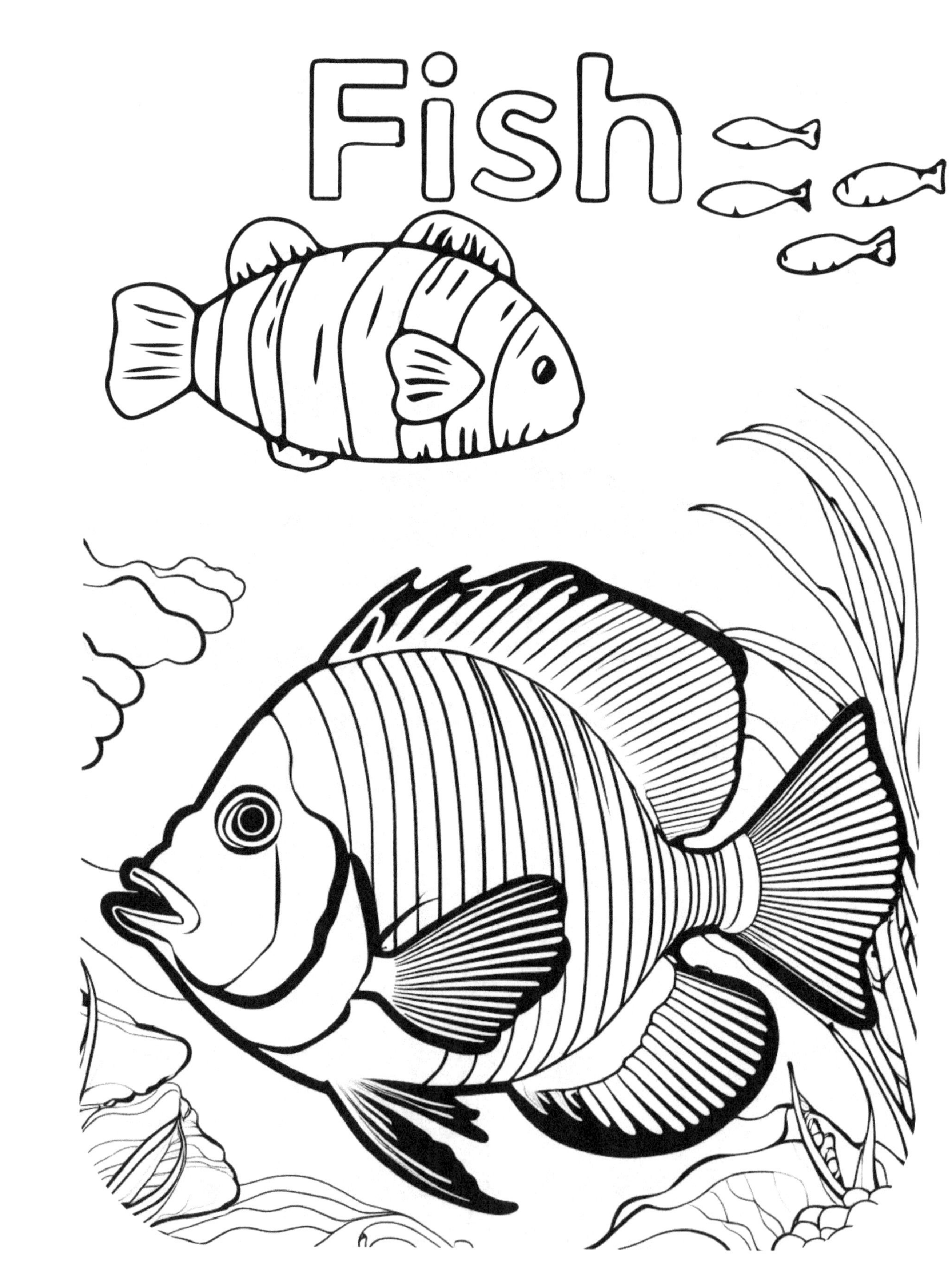

# Pescado

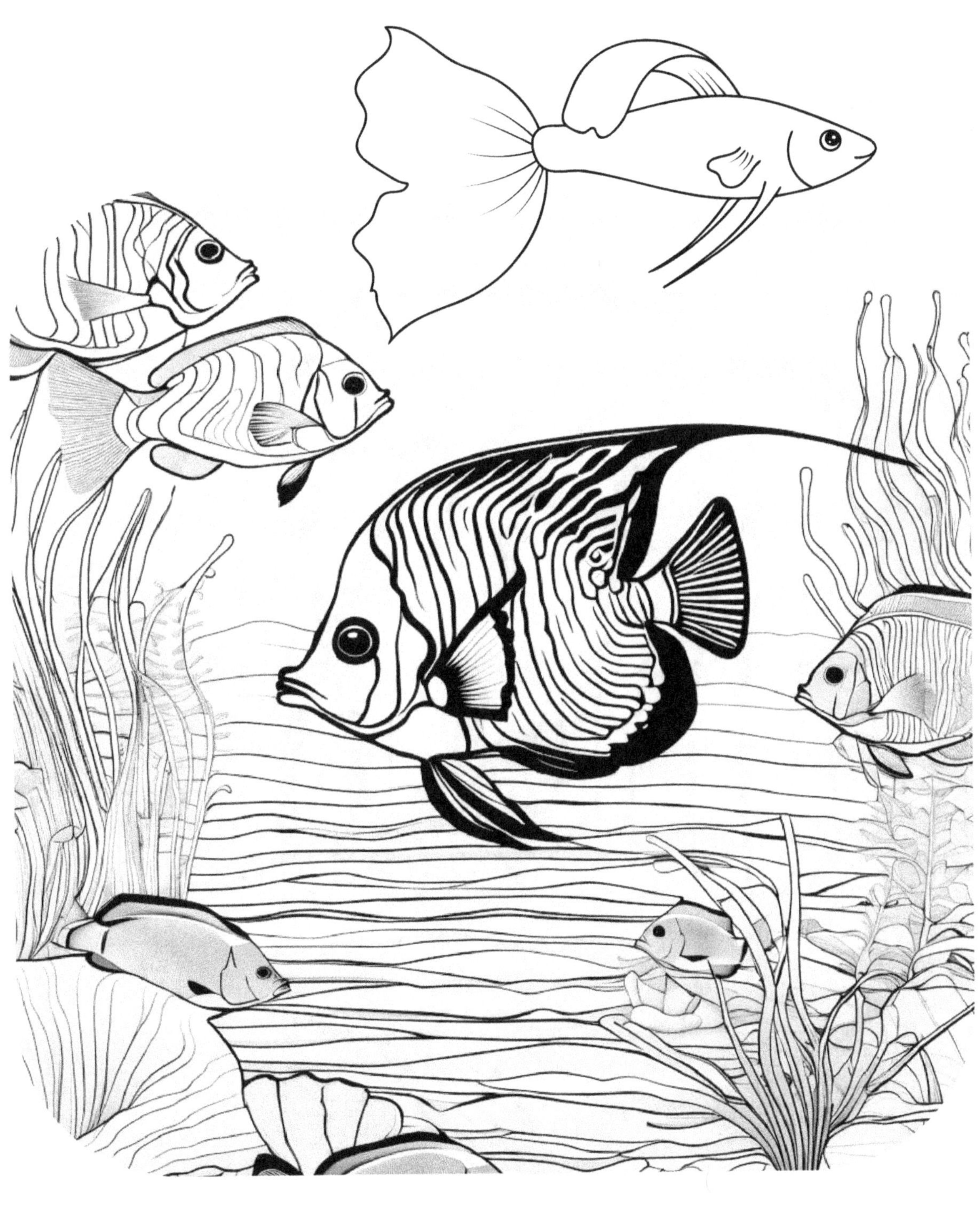

# Pez

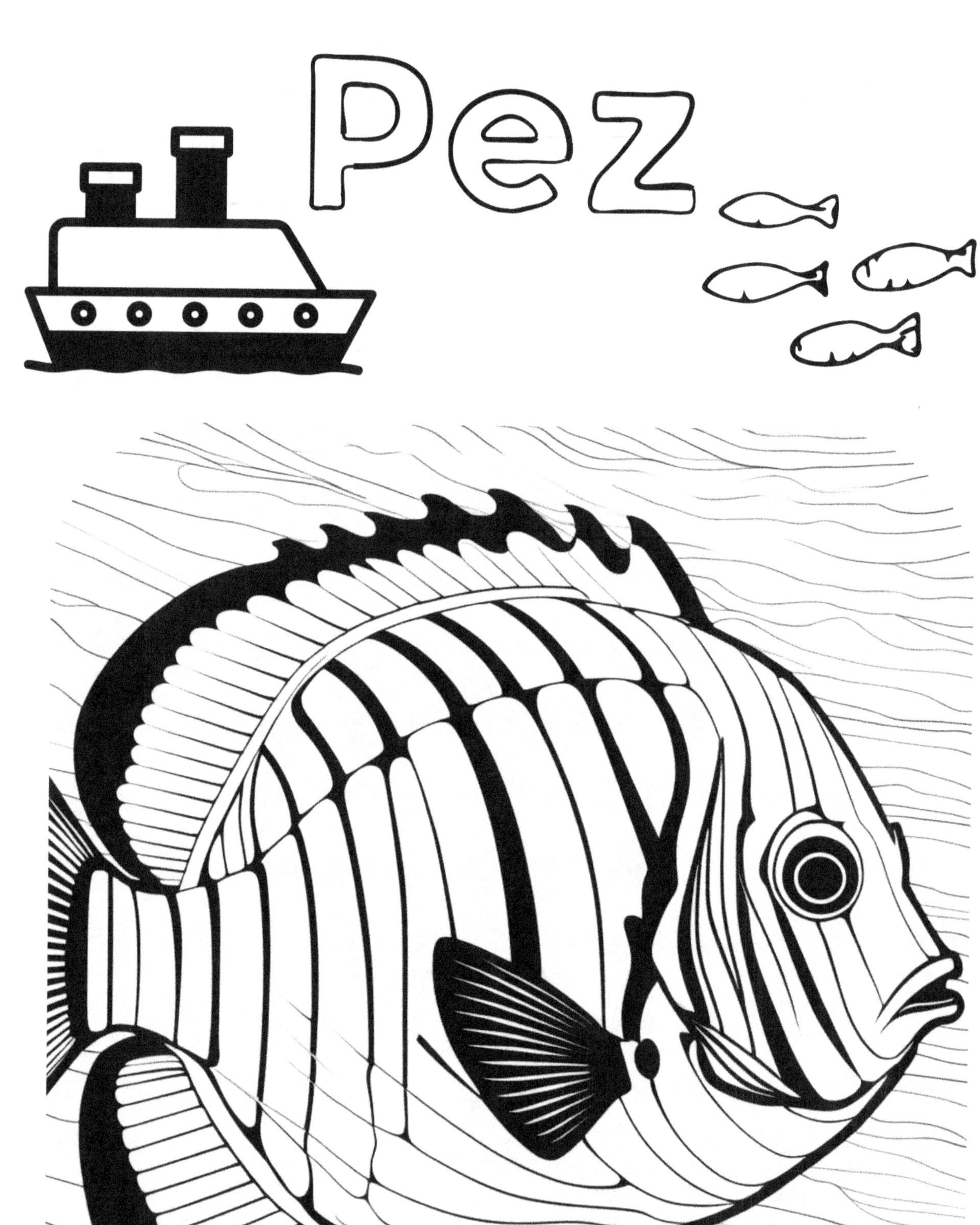

# Fishing

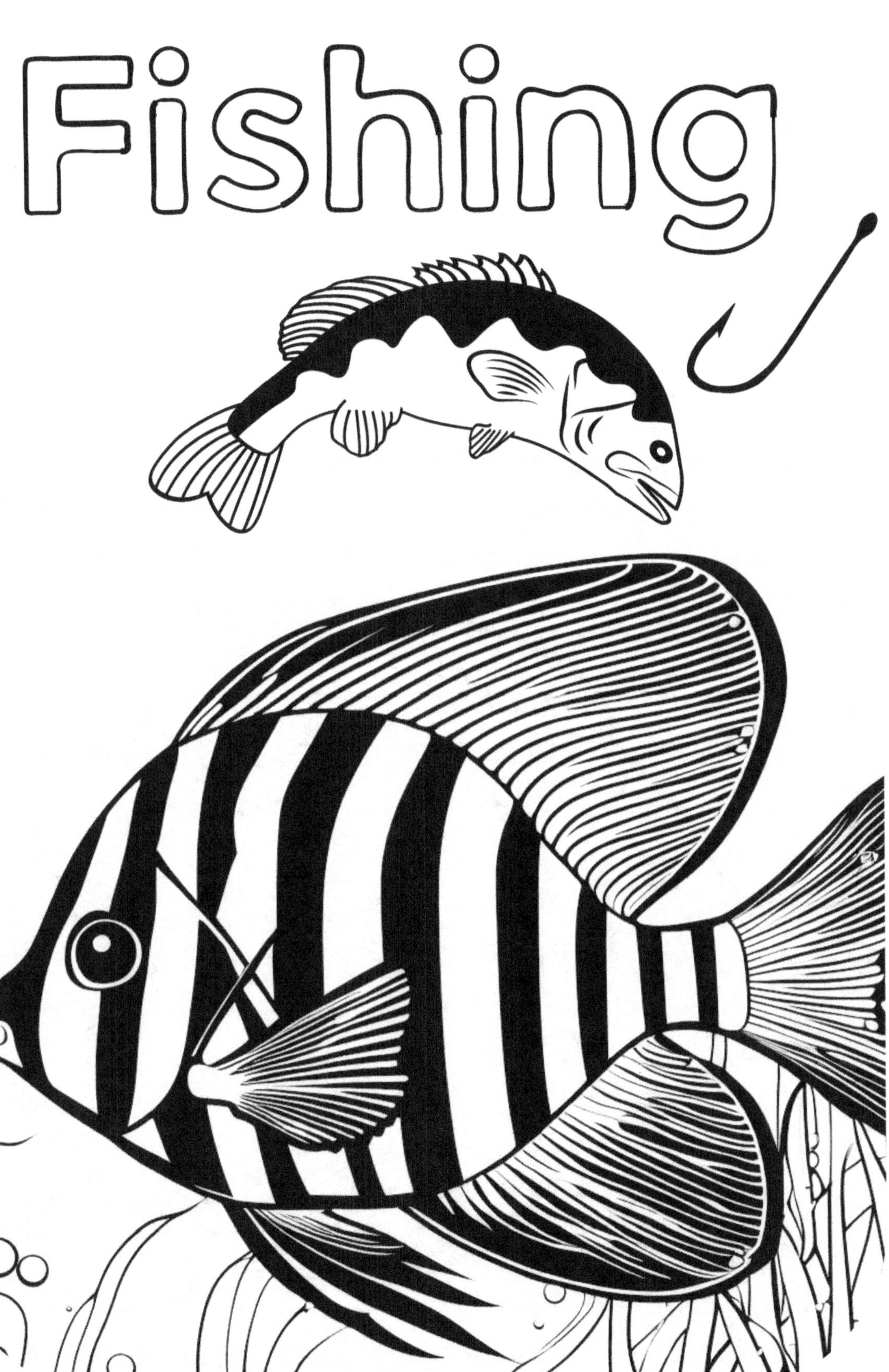

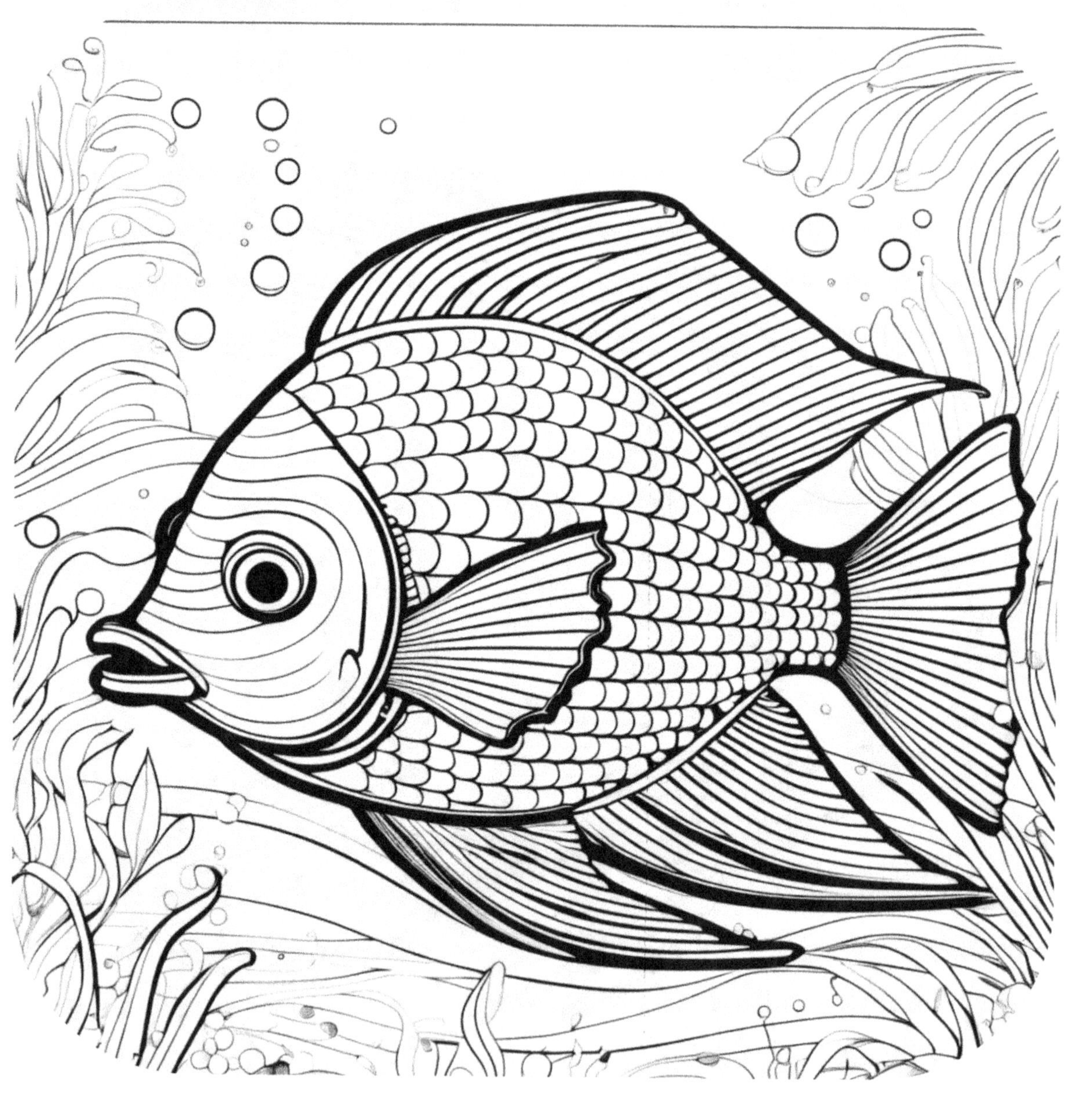
Pesca

# Aquarium

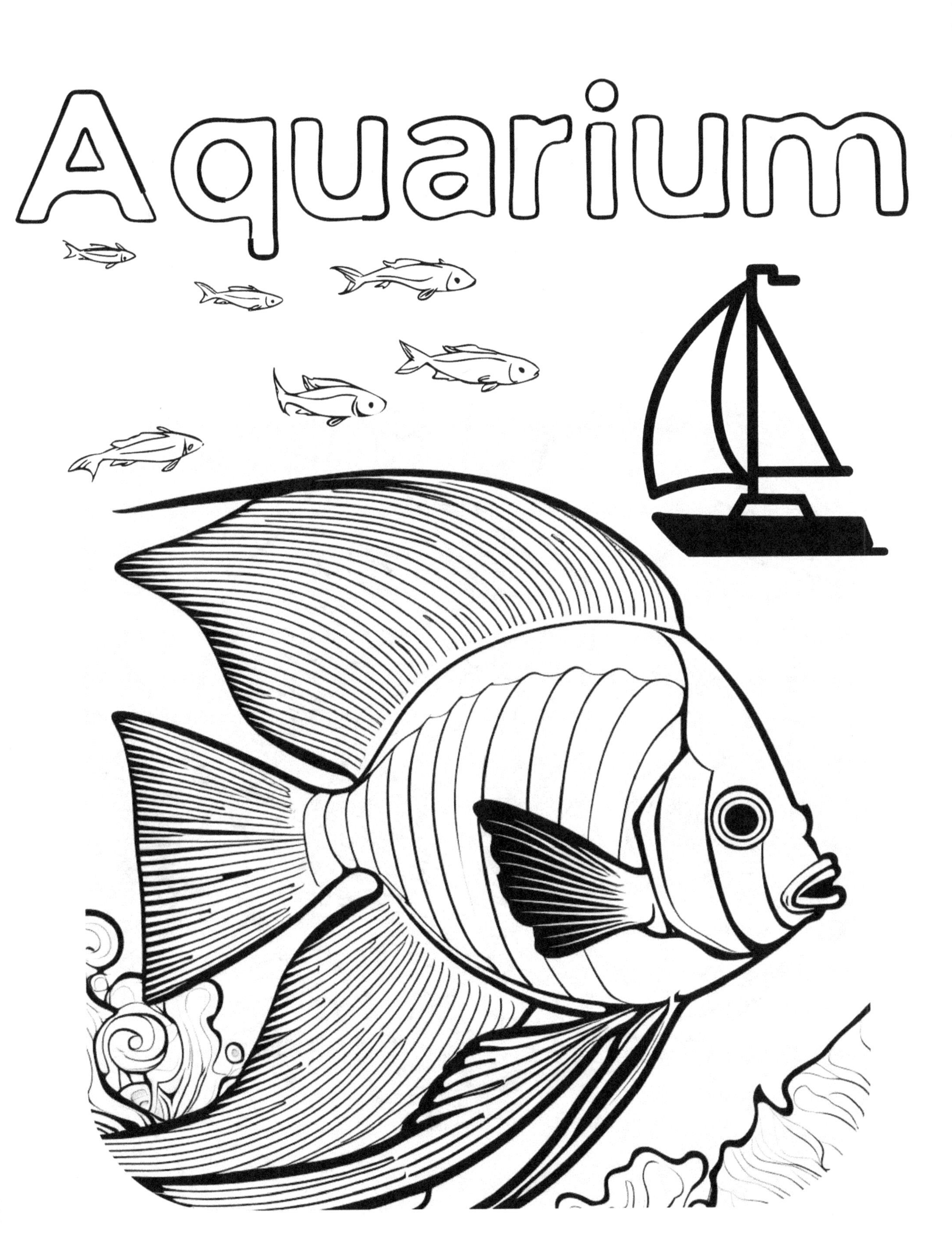

# Acuario

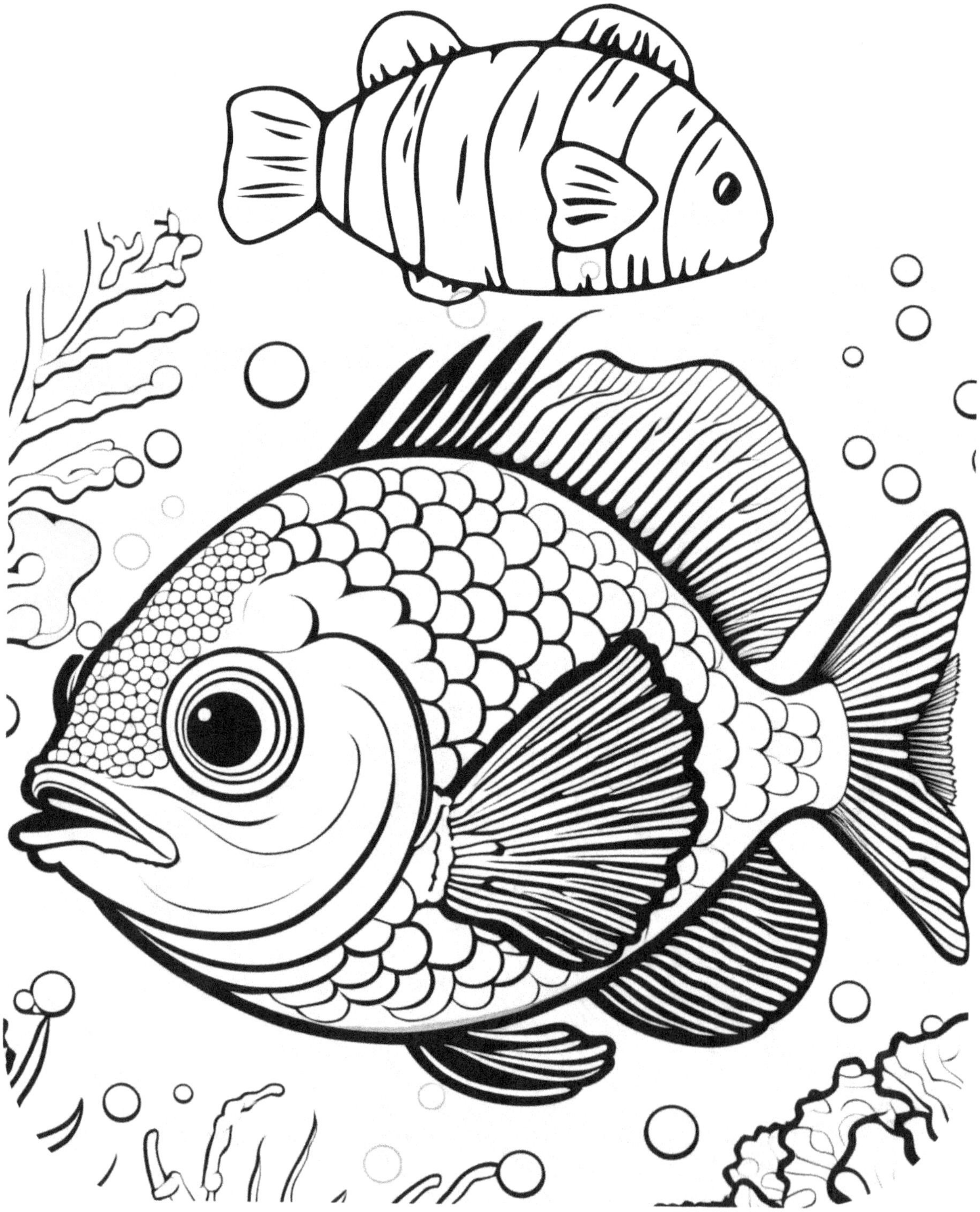

# Fish tank

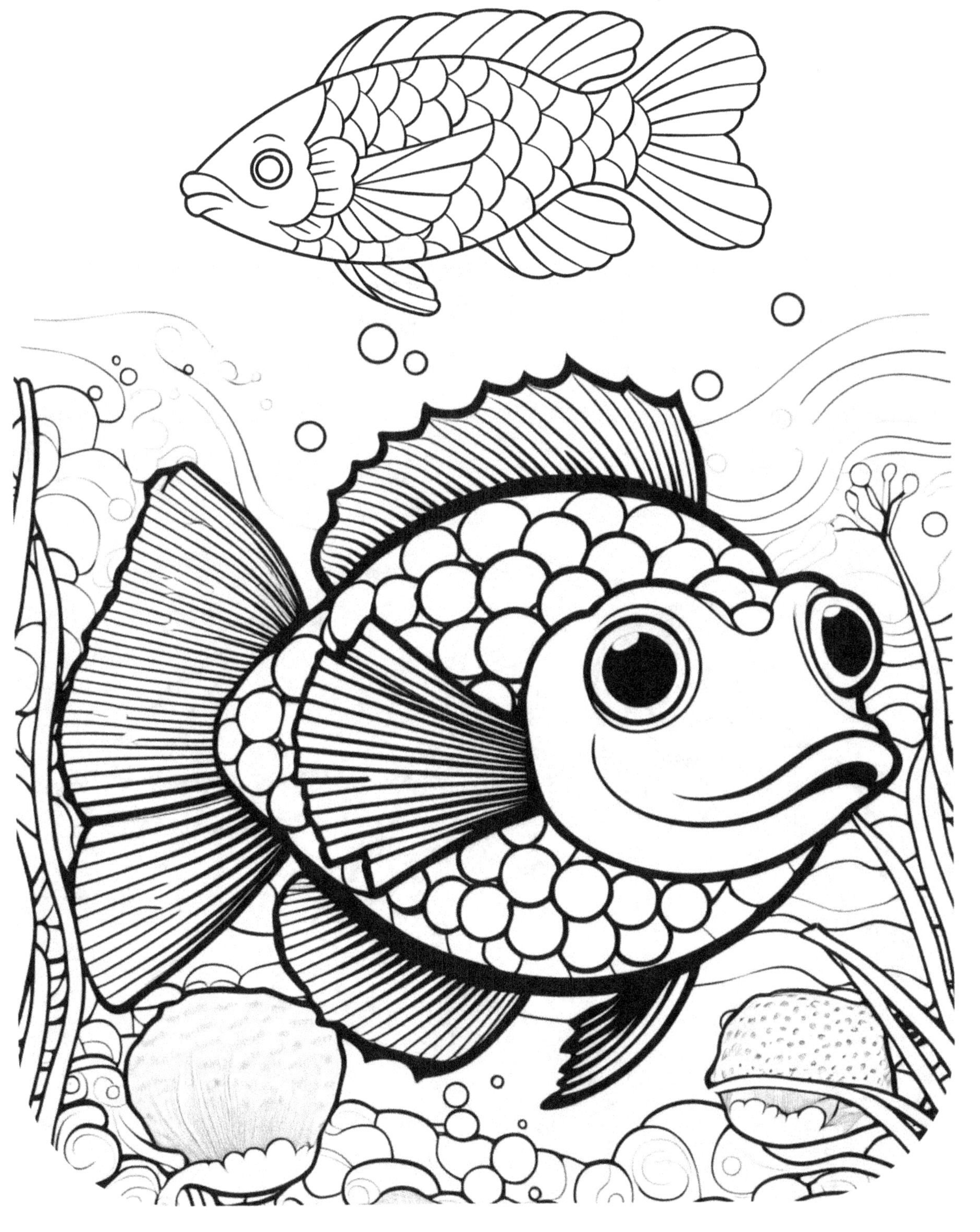

# Turtle

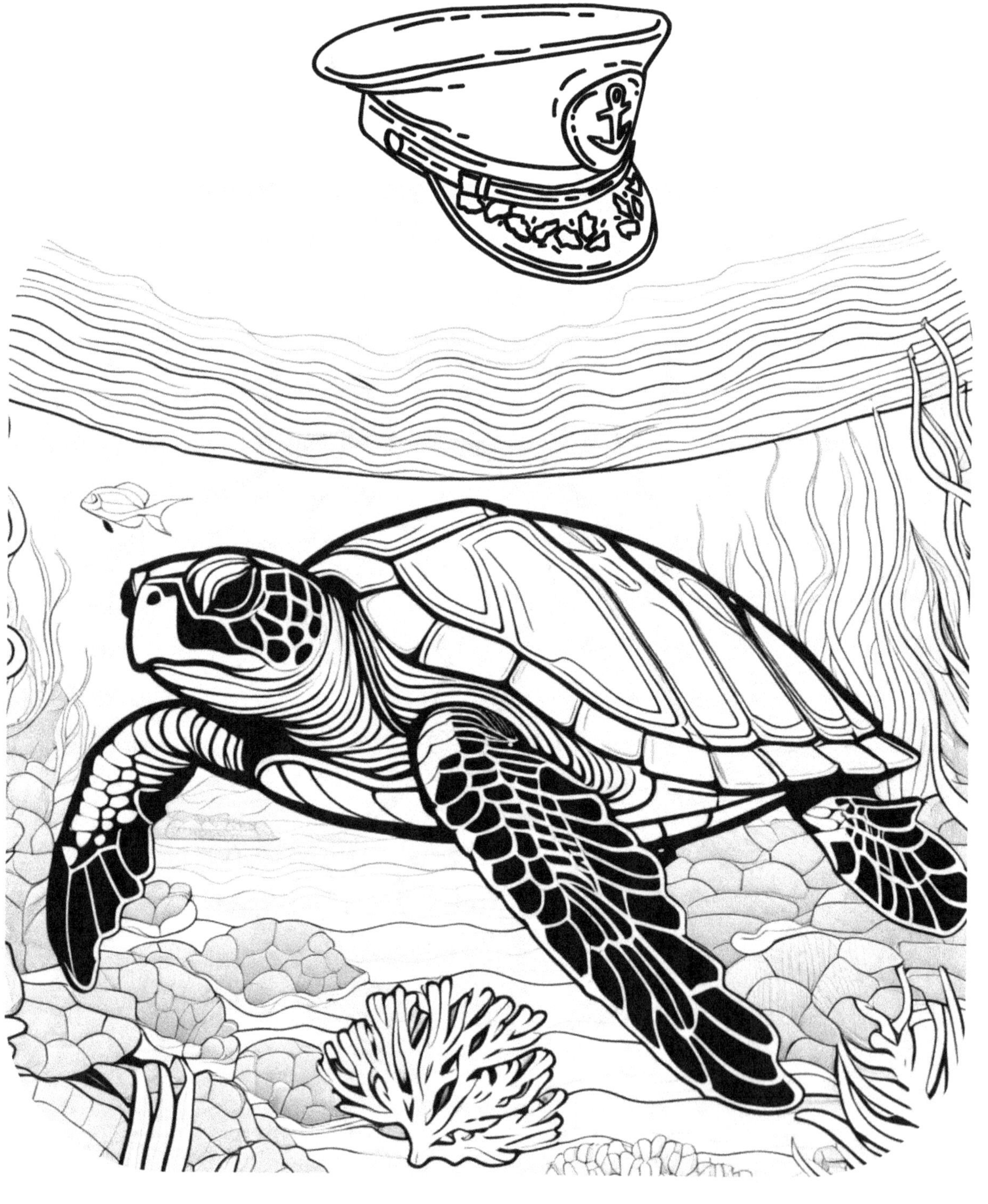

# Tortuga

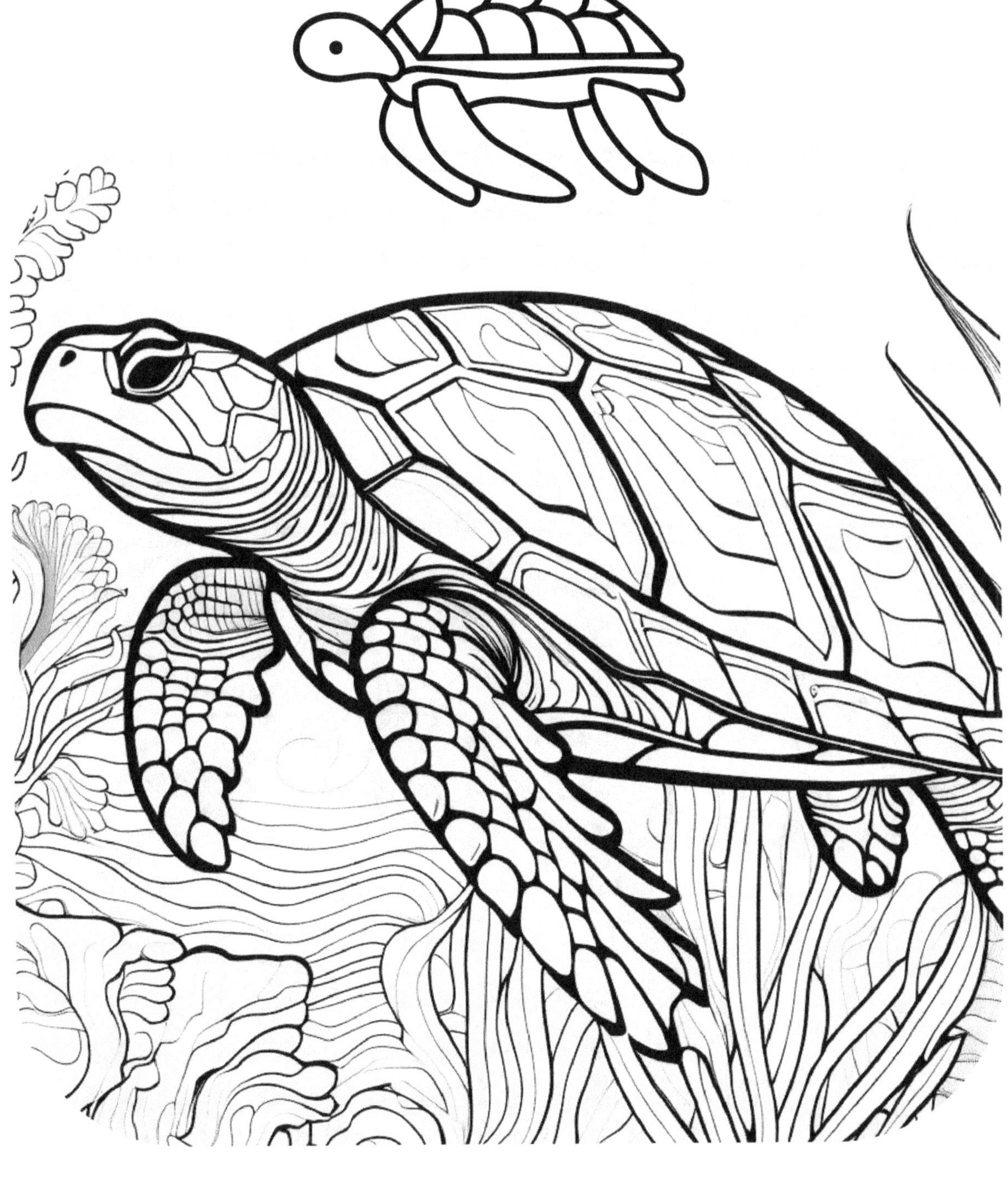

# Tortoise

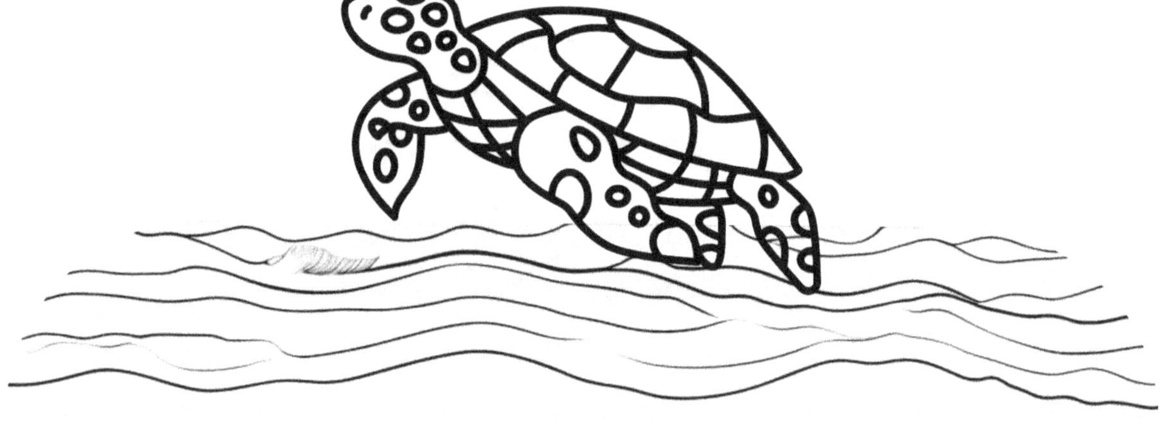

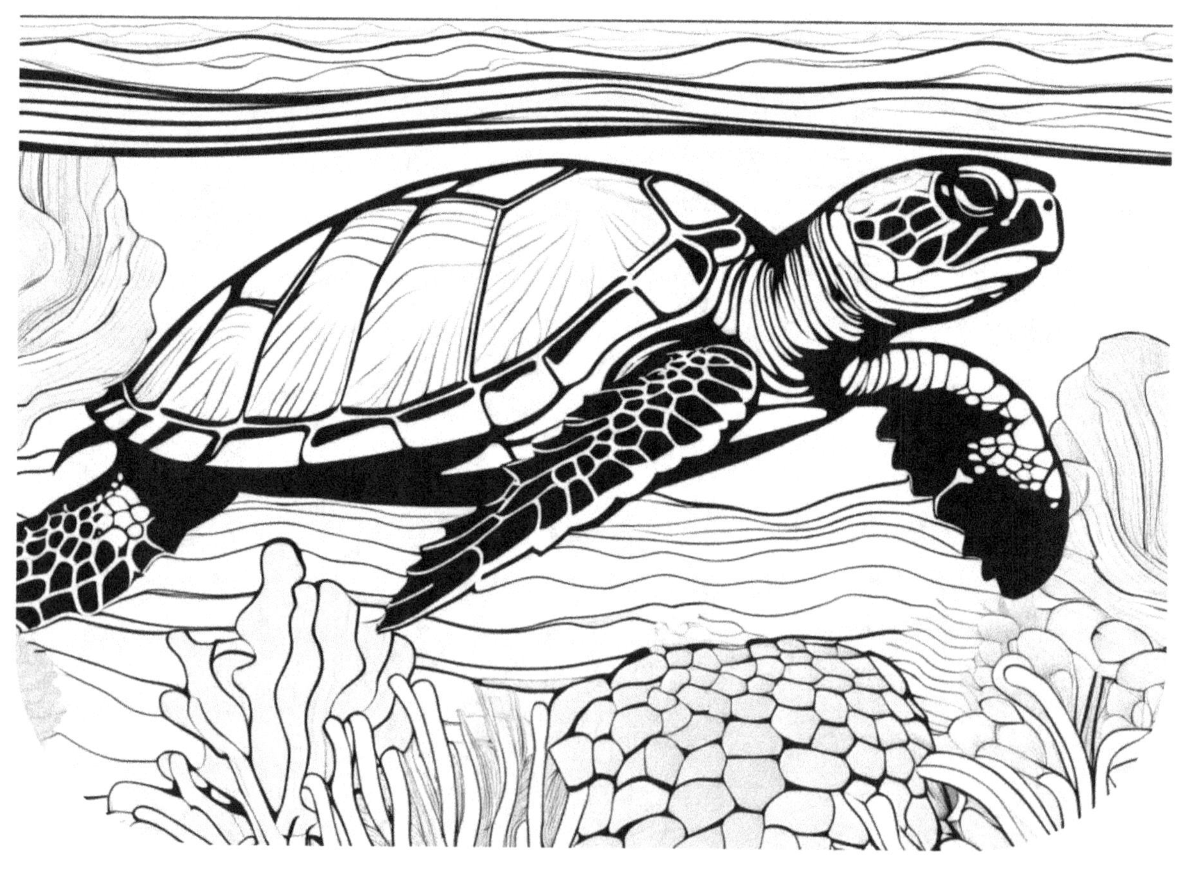

# Lobster

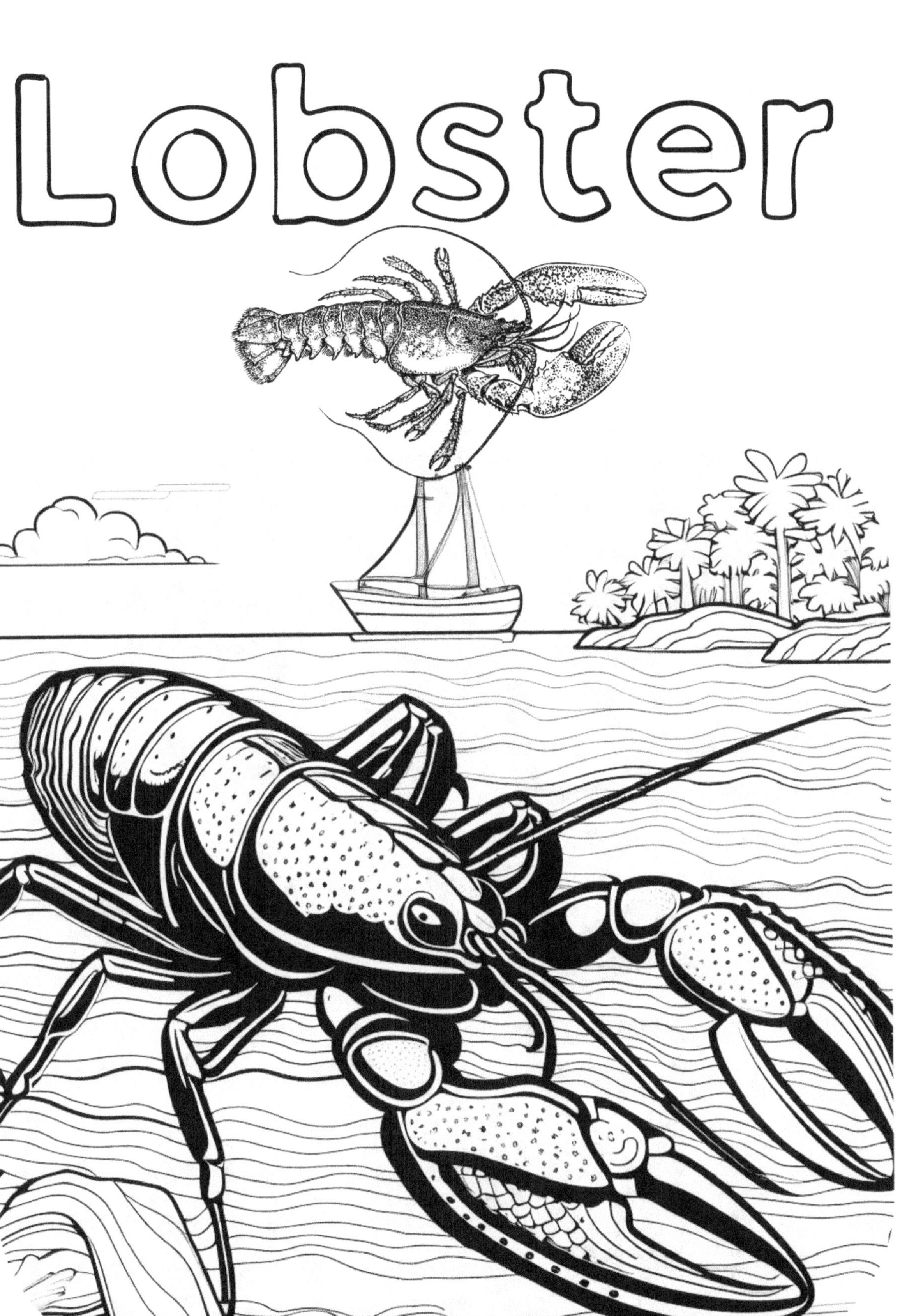

# Langosta

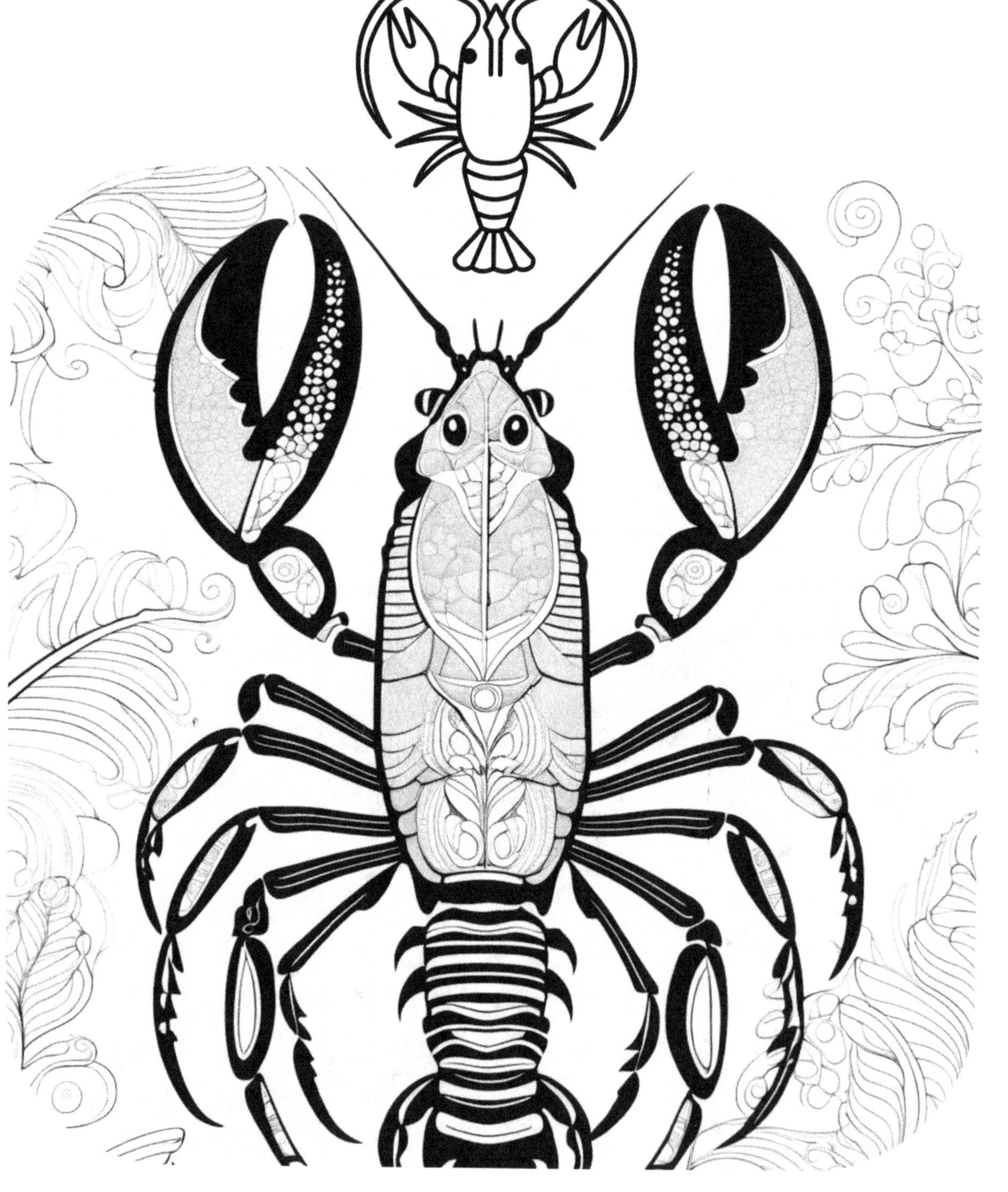

# Crab

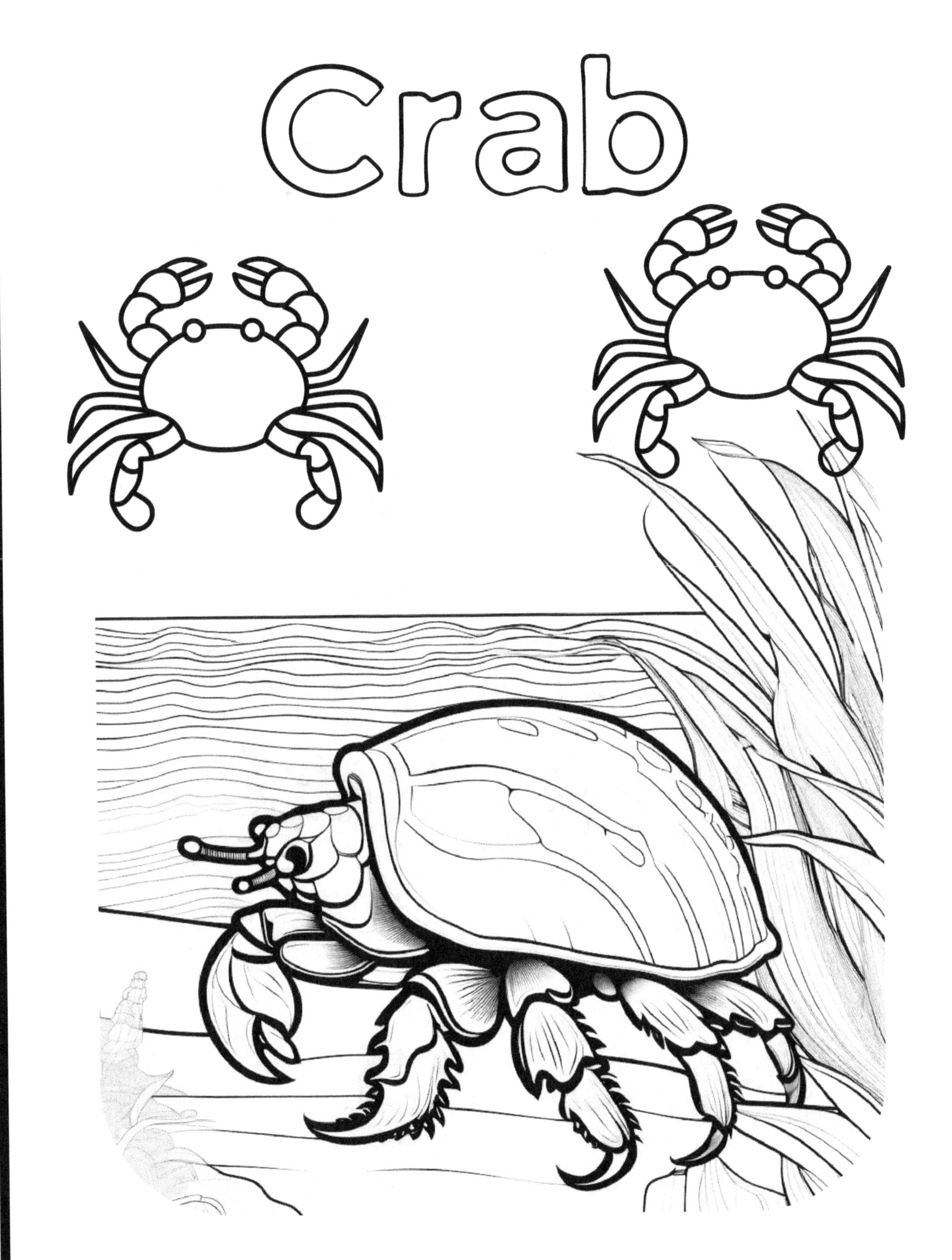

# Cangrejo

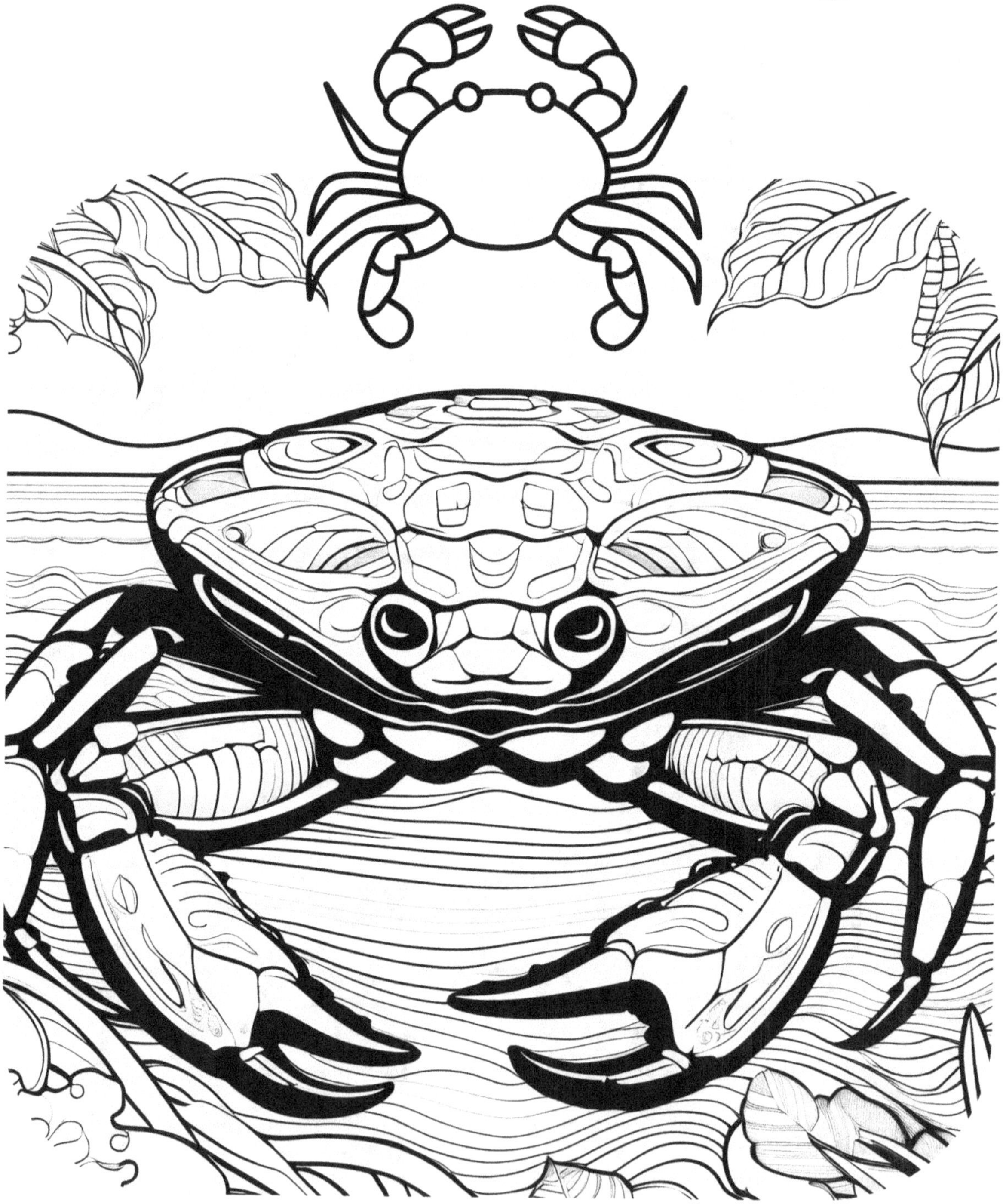

# Octopus

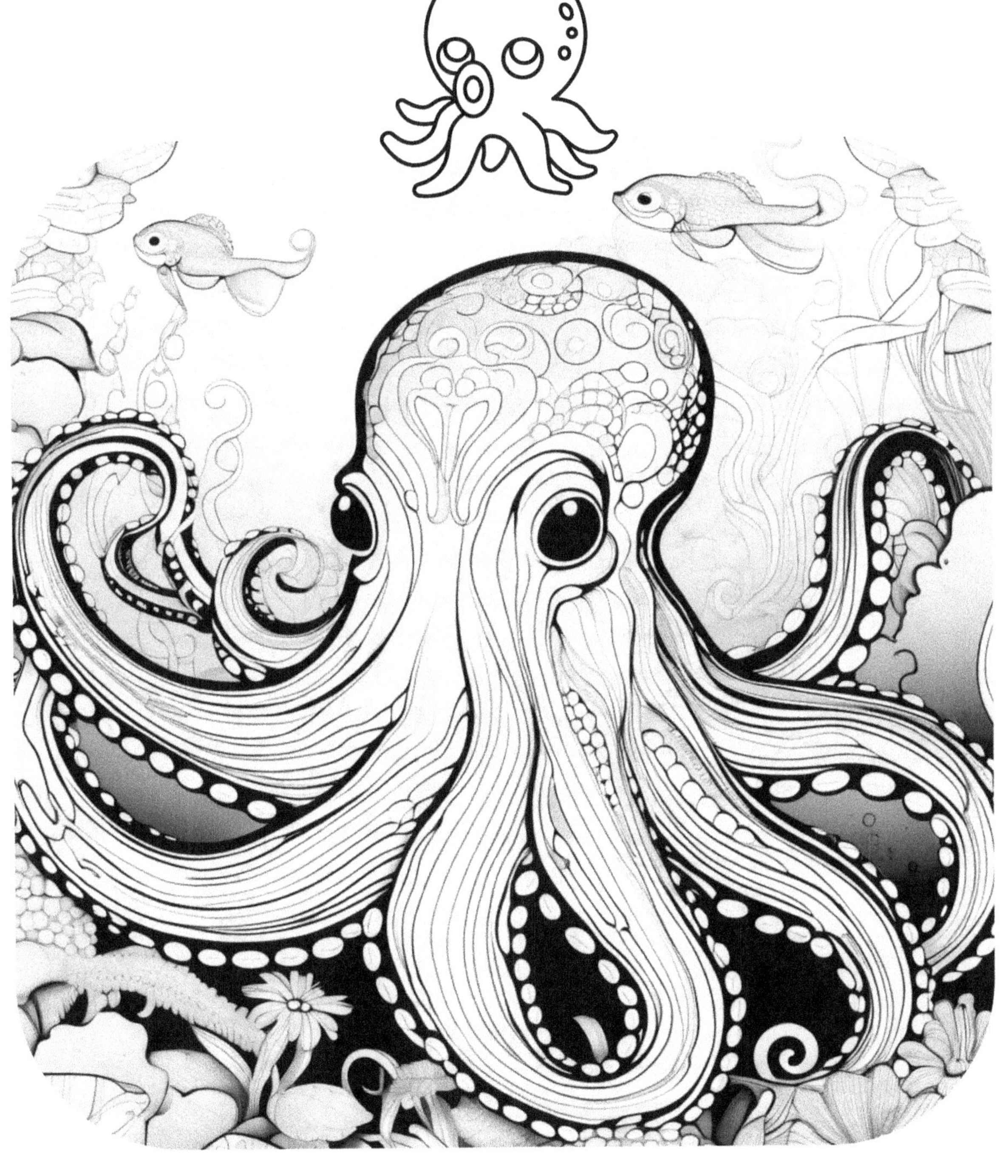

# Pulpo

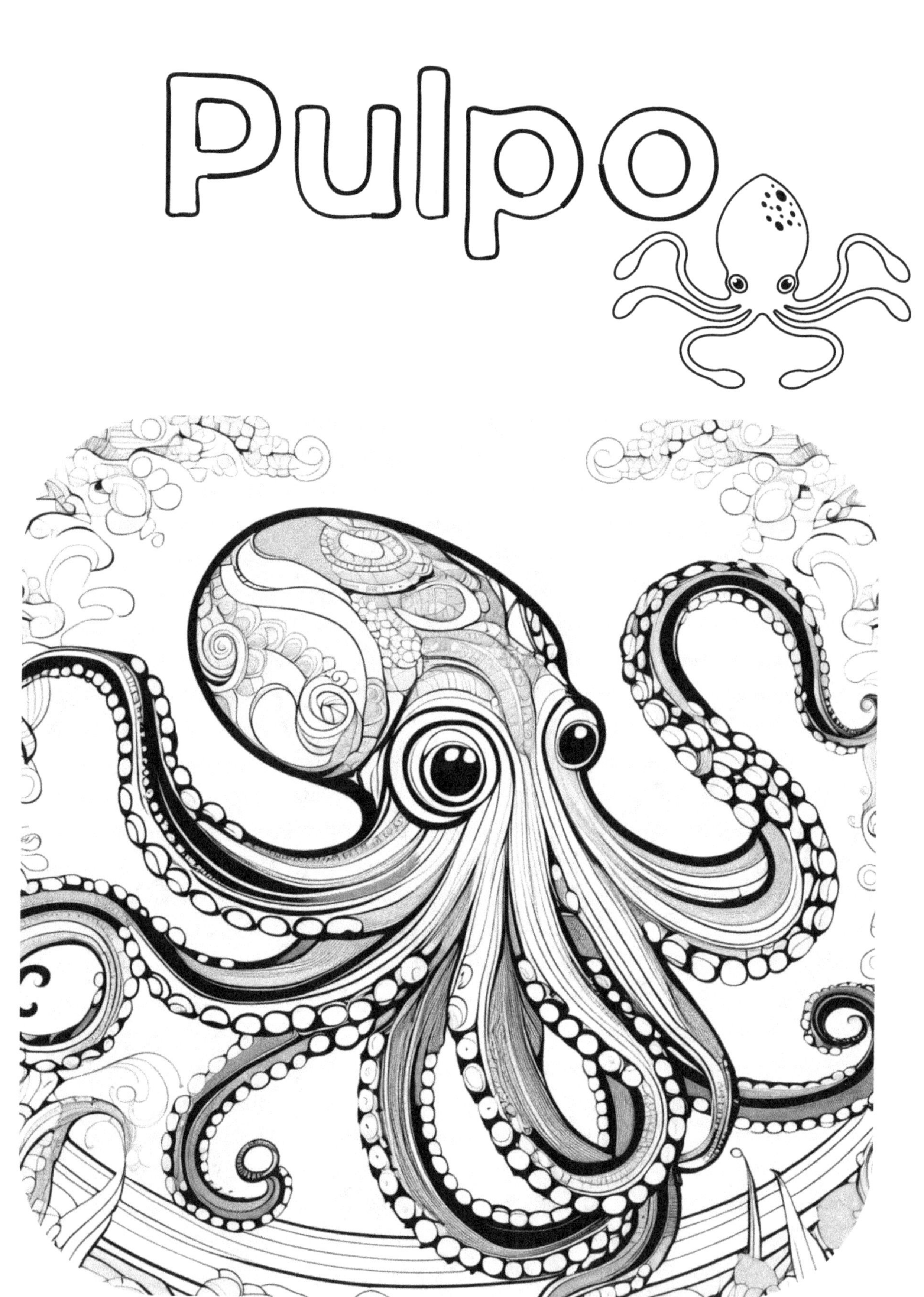

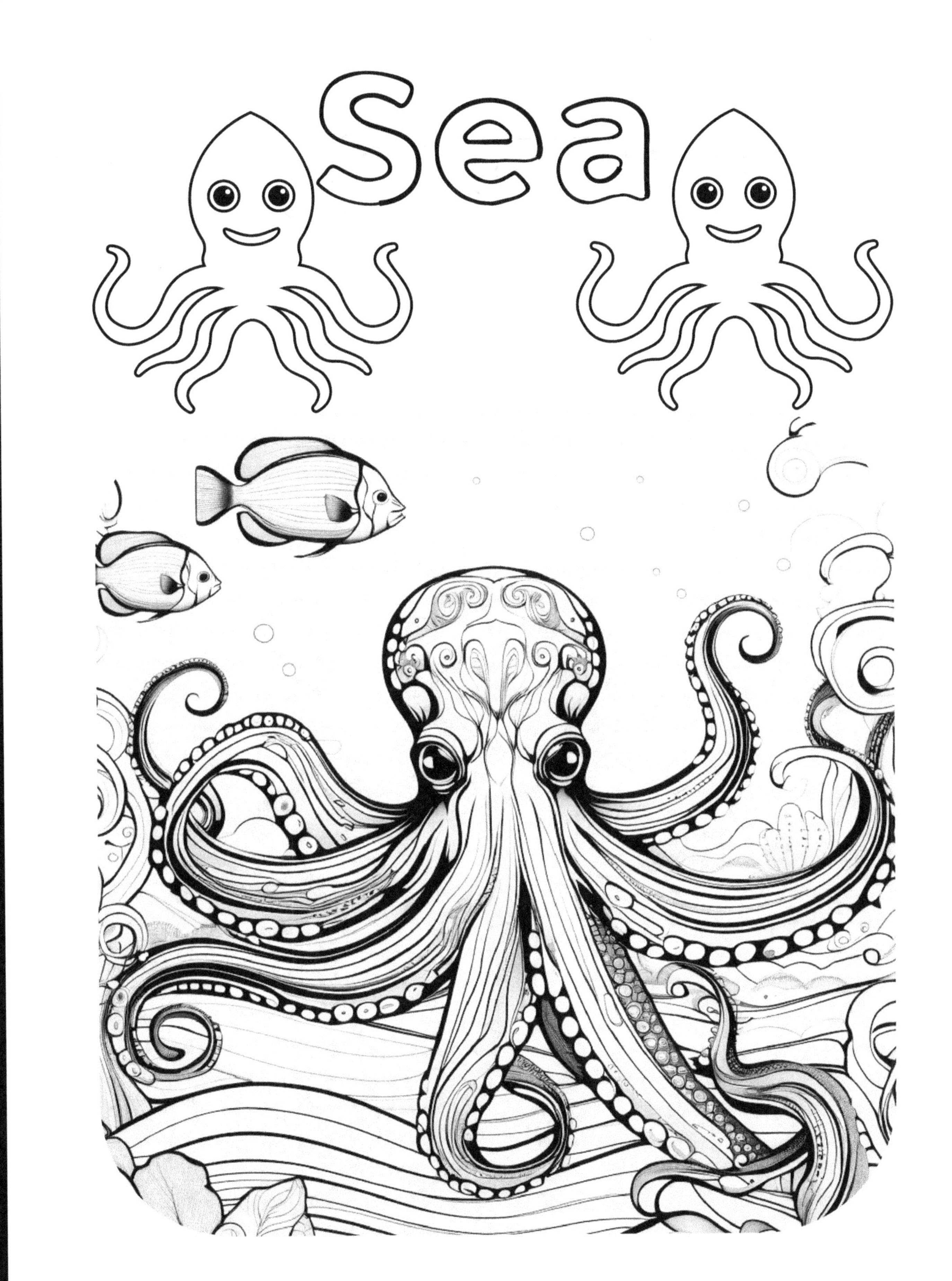

Sea

# Diver

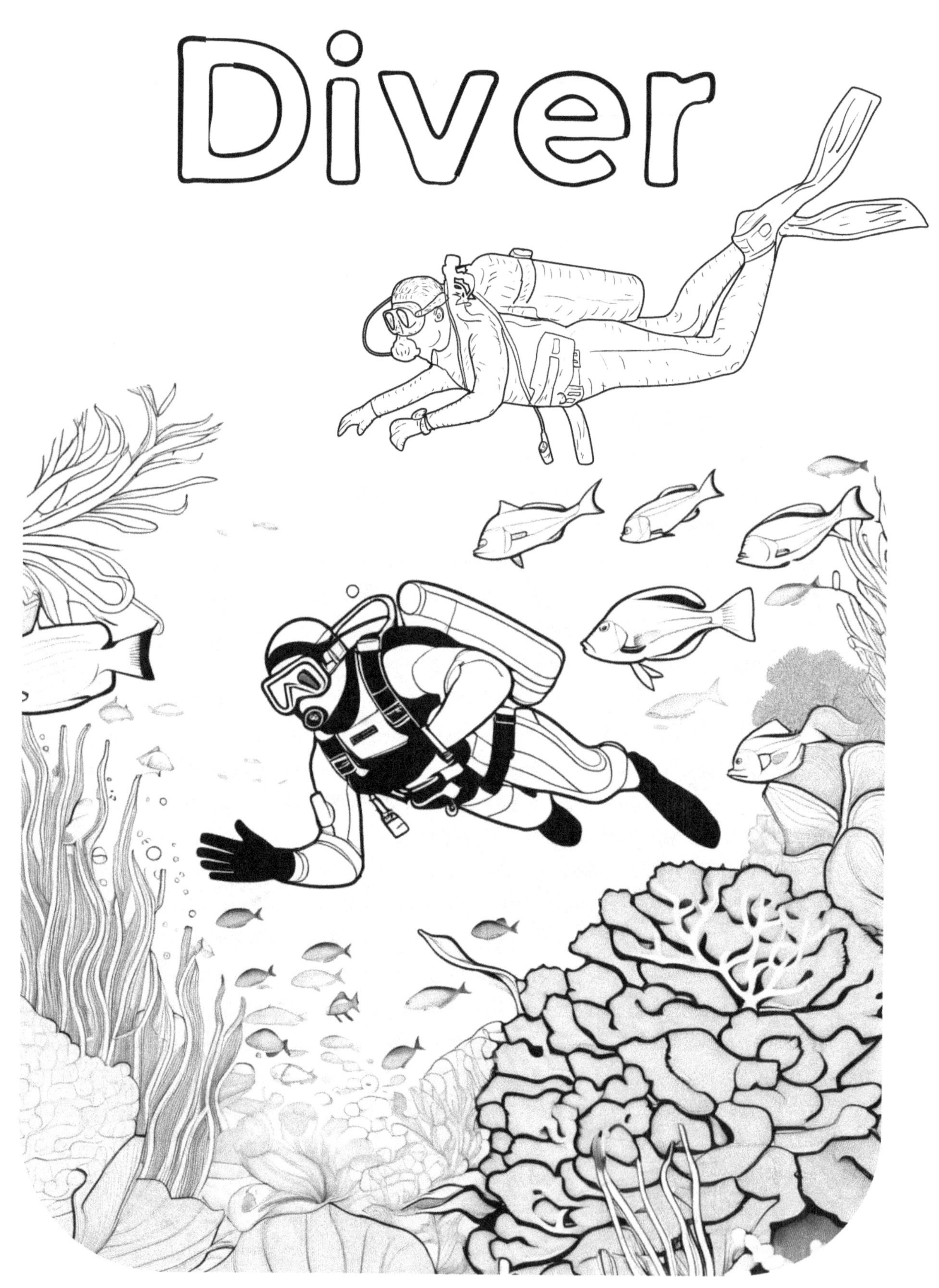

# Buceador

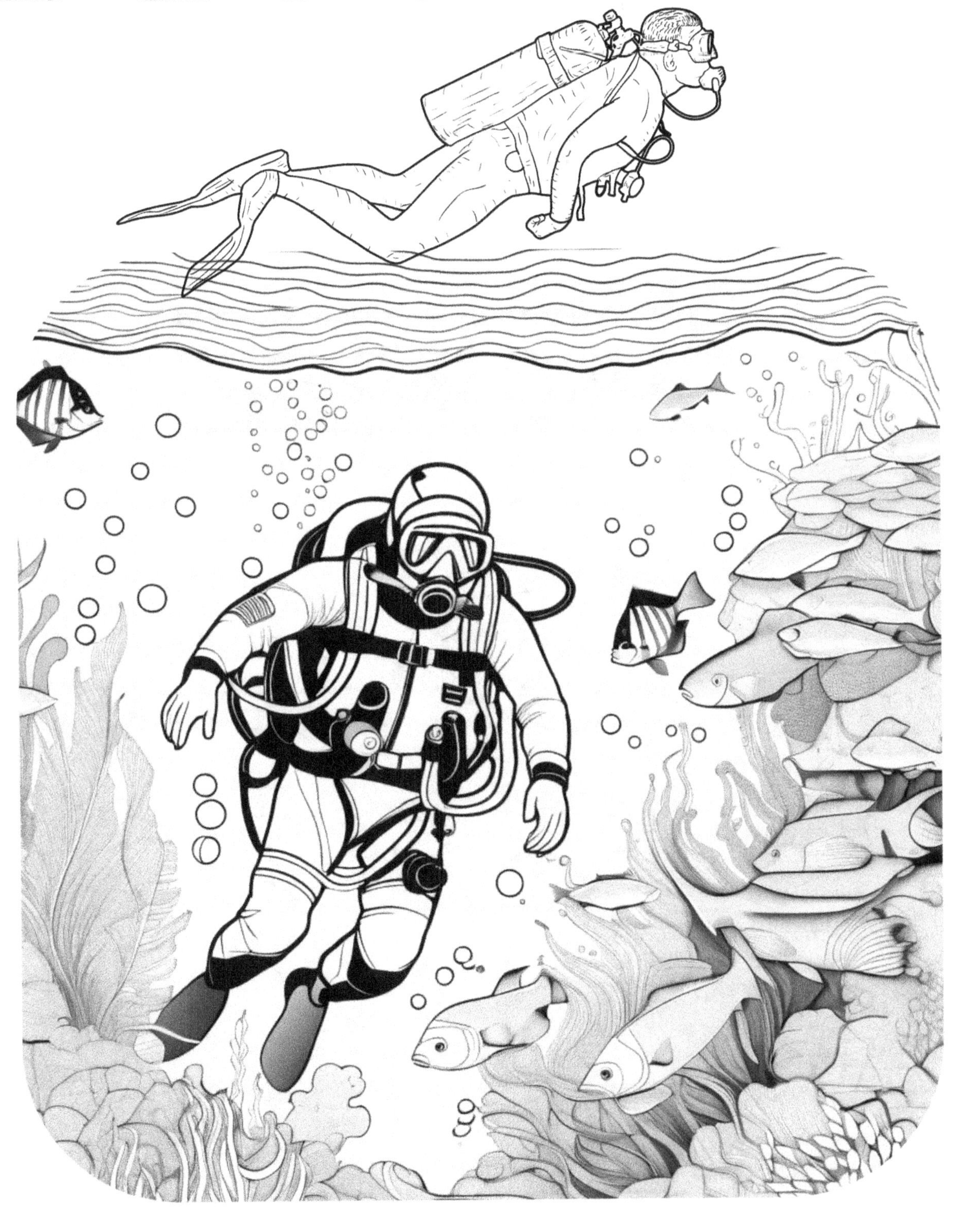

# In the sea

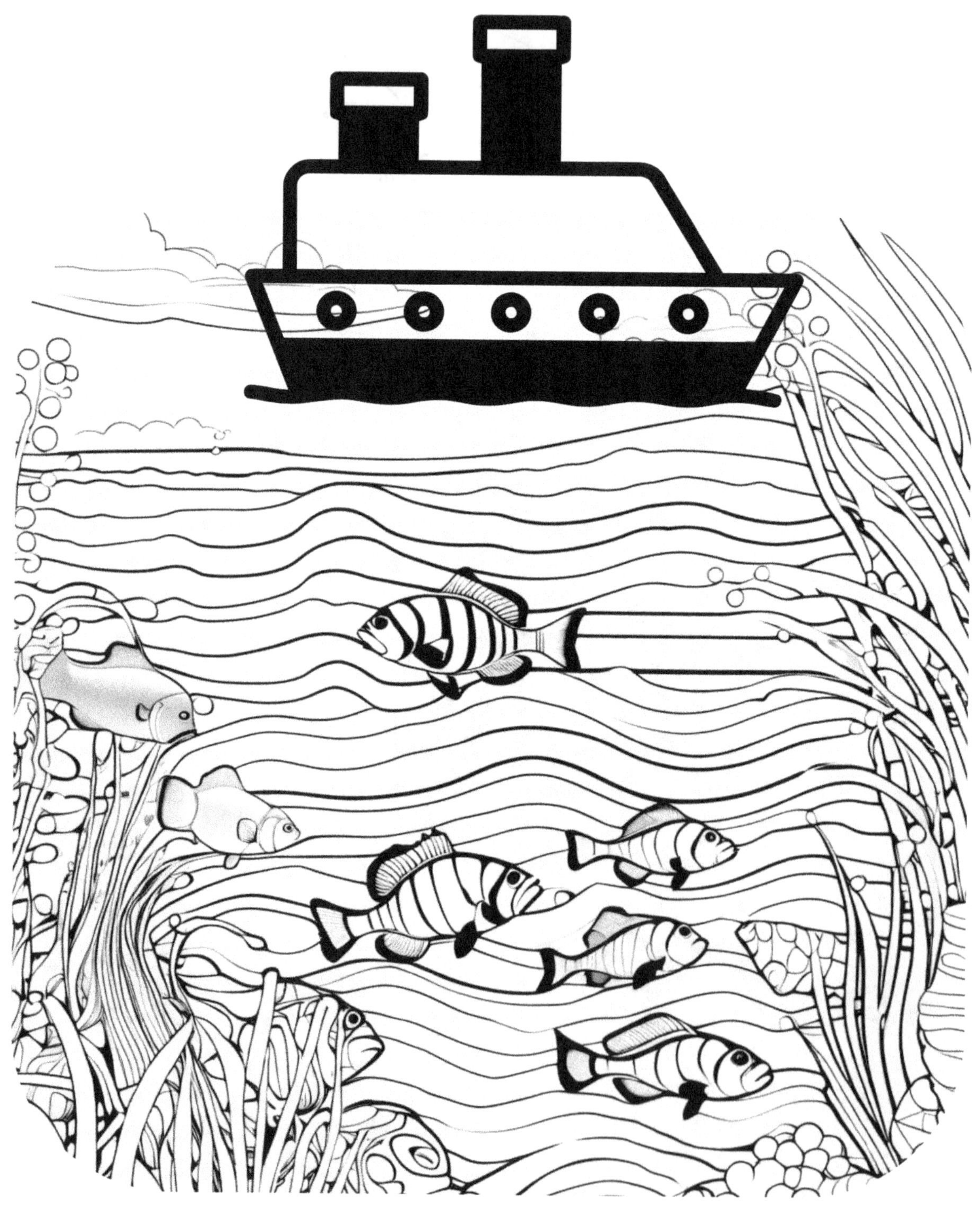

# En el mar

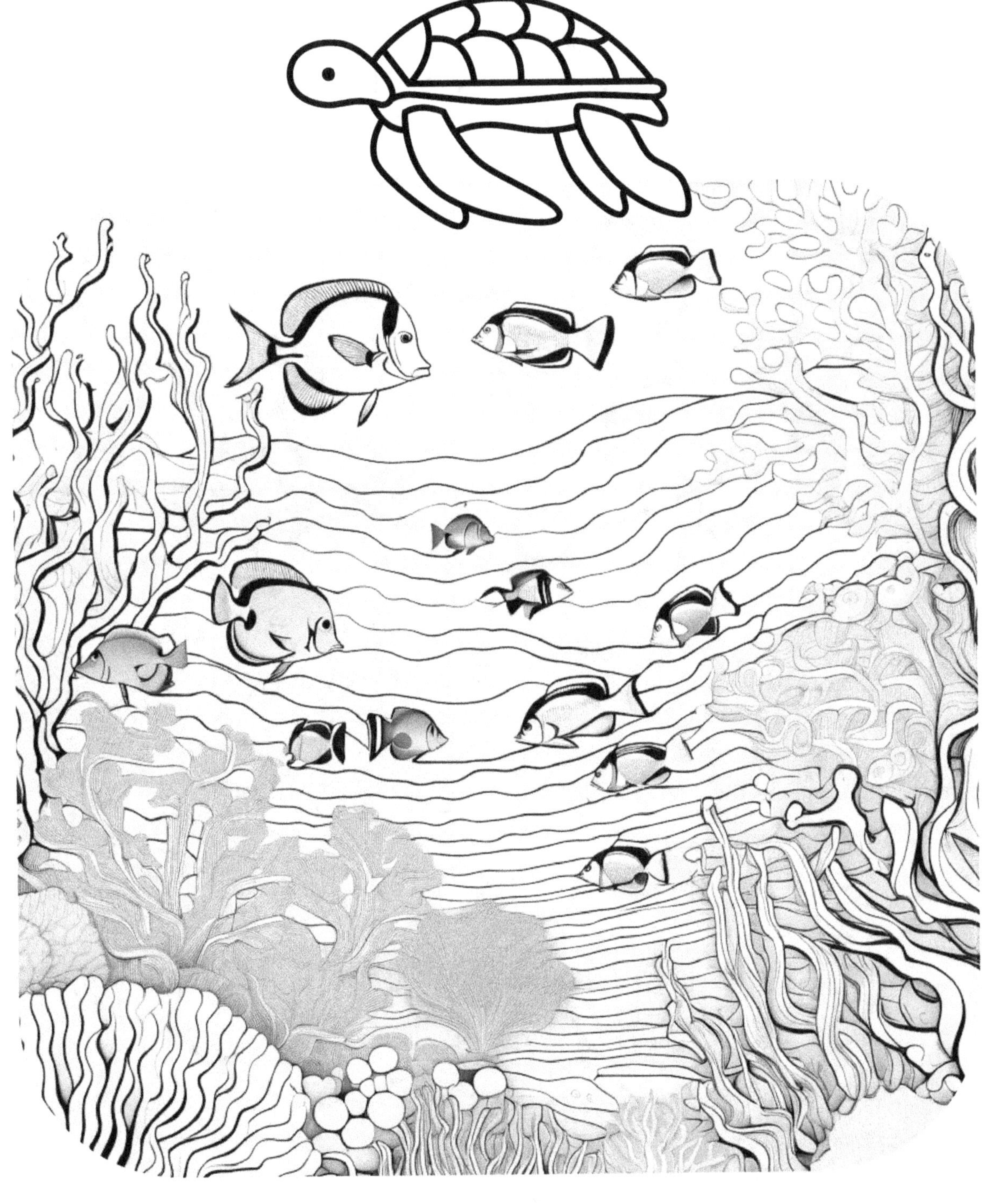

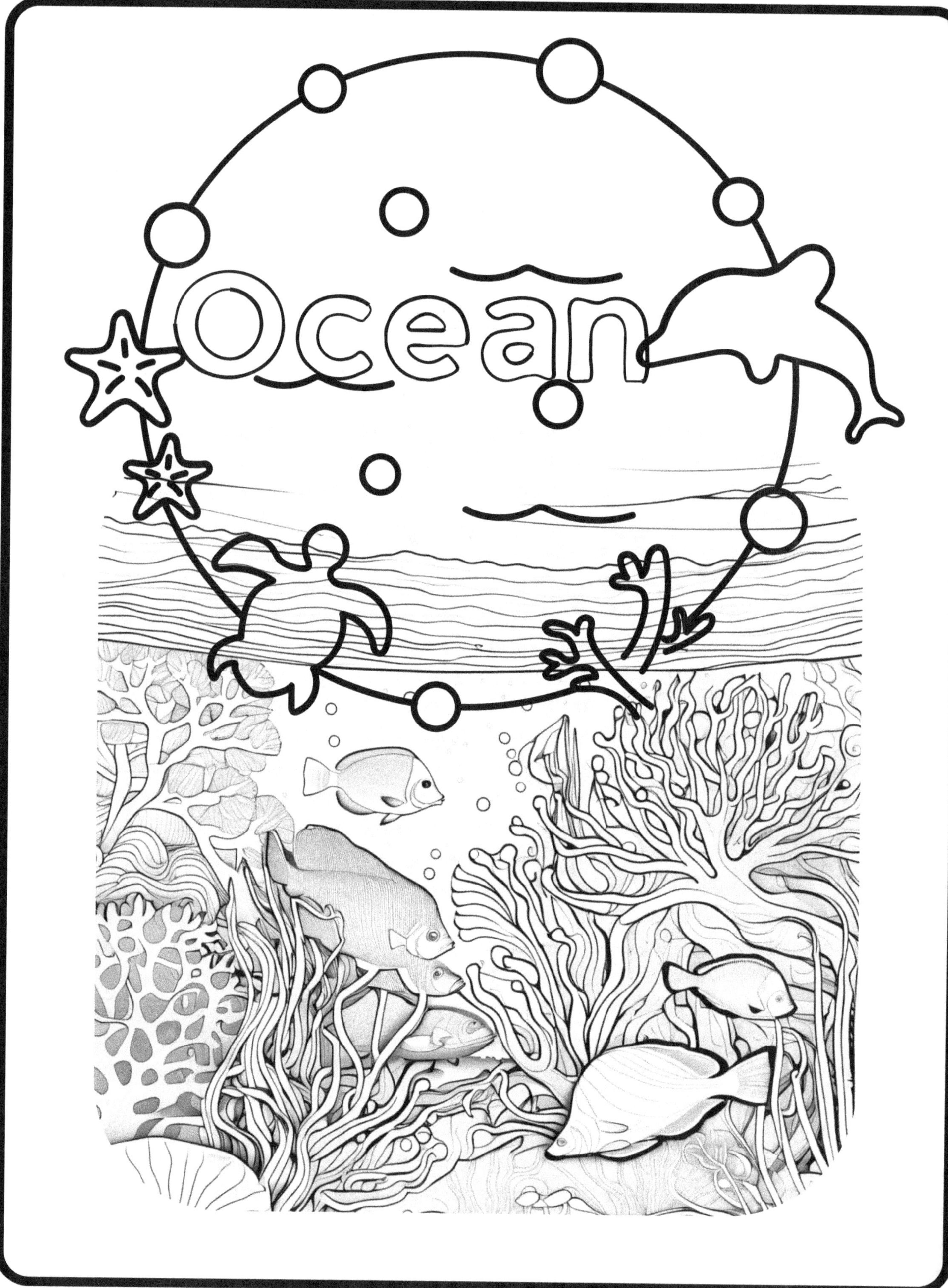
Ocean

# Oceano

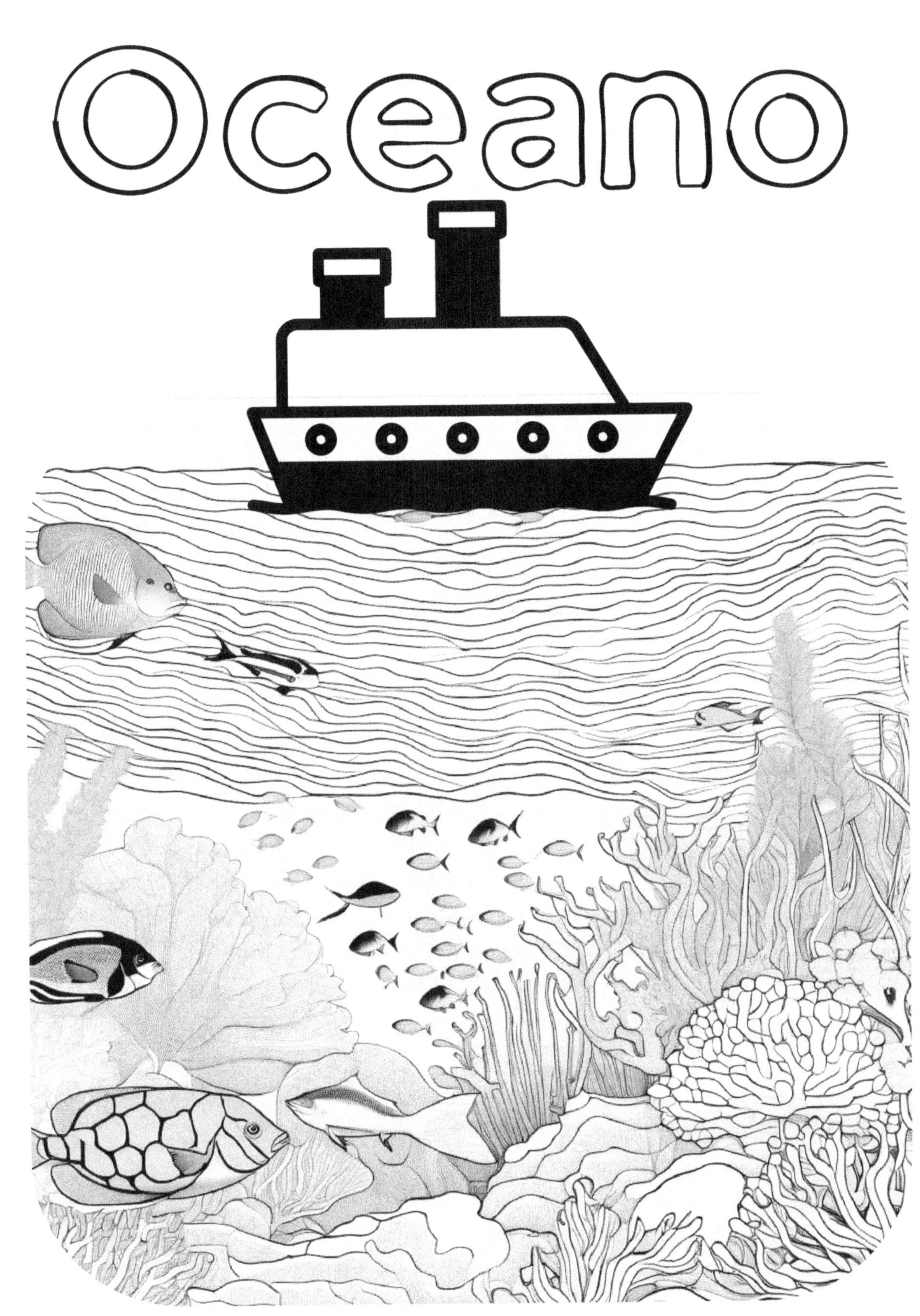

# Ship

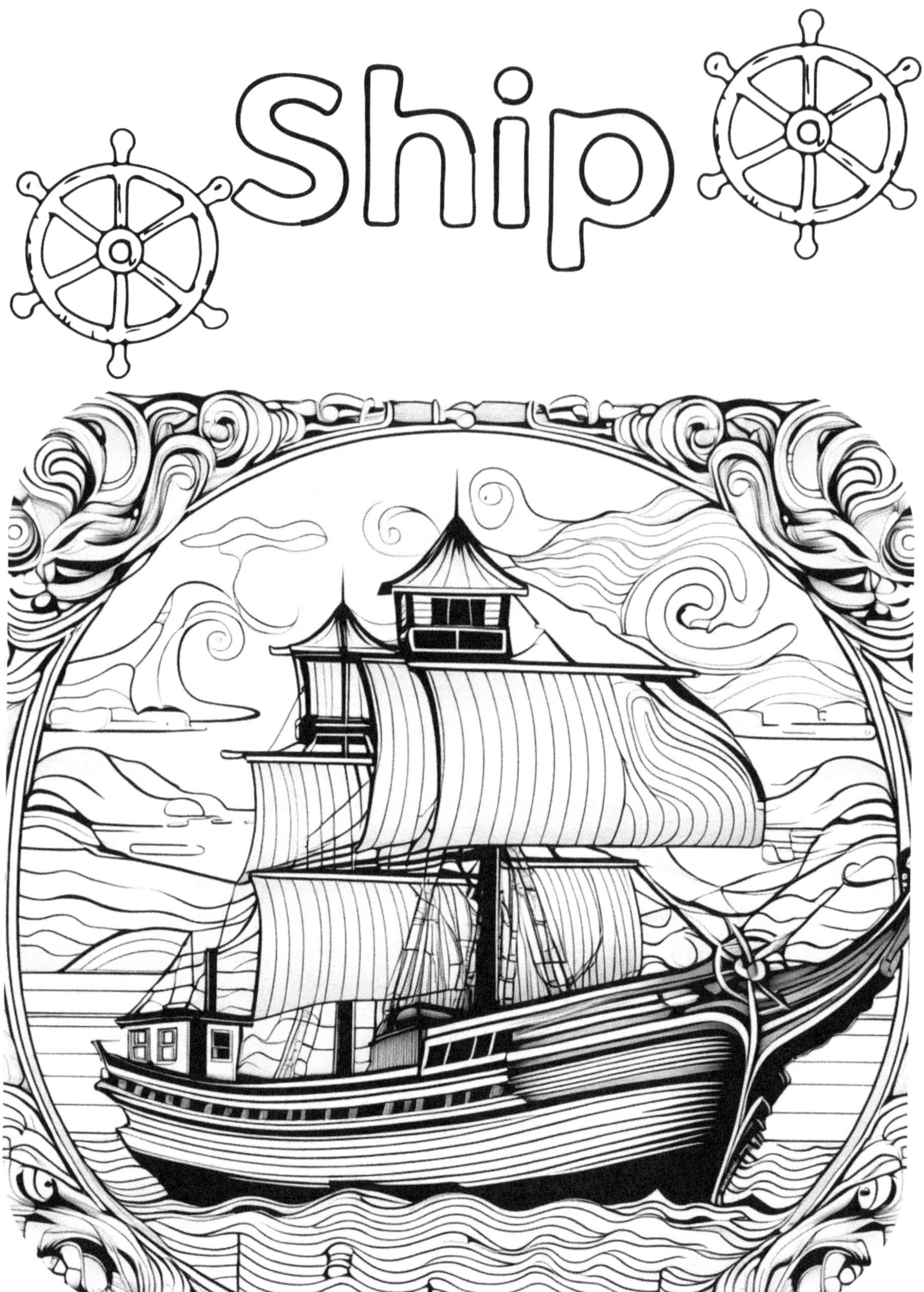